ARTIFICIAL

IMAGINATION

An Insider's Glimpse into the Hi-Tech world of Silicon Valley, Seattle and more

A book by Kalpanik S.
Photography by Colin Zheng and others
Edited by Neha Talreja

Published in the United States by The Center
of Artificial Imagination, Inc.

www.Artificial-Imagination.com

CENTER OF
Artificial
Imagination inc.

Library of Congress Control Number: 2008923070

Published in the United States by The Center of Artificial Imagination, Inc.

www.Artificial-Imagination.com

Acknowledgements: Many photos included in the text were taken by Dr. Colin Zheng, a graduate student at University of Washington at the time.

For Sonia

Seattle University, Photo by Dr. Colin Zheng

Contents

Foreword

Technology is all brain, no heart, all cold logic, and no warm soul.

That's what we tell ourselves, anyway, and that's what our art and our literature have been saying to us for centuries, in everything from H.G. Wells to Philip K. Dick, from Frankenstein to The Matrix. Computers, particularly, are seen as downright dangerous, and artificial intelligence is something to be feared. That's the message the larger culture absorbs from HAL9000 in 2001: A Space Odyssey, or from SkyNet in The Terminator series, or the Replicants in Blade Runner, or... You get the idea.

By extension, we tend to view those who work in these fields with a bit of suspicion. When I was an undergraduate we, the Humanities majors, were all convinced that "Techies" were people who couldn't identify with human beings. They kept odd hours; they spoke in a language we couldn't decipher. They understand something we do not, as our logic ran. Therefore, they are suspicious and strange; we are as standoffish to the people who worked with the machines as we were to the machines themselves.

Small wonder, then, that this gem of a book comes as such a delightful surprise. It reminds us that technology could not exist were it not for boundless creativity, and it does this in such a way as to also remind us that without that very same creativity, there would be no art, no poetry. The mysteries of technology are the mysteries of the human mind and soul. The desire to create comes from the same place.

But there is so much more here than that, so very much more. Under the guise of an AI creative-writing program -- "Kalpanik S" -- we are taken on a journey through time and space and the musings of a man with multiple identities: tech-sector whiz kid, immigrant in a new land, husband, father, human being trying to understand his place in the world. There is so much here that is universal. "Crossing the Median" is the story of every father. "Welcome to Seattle" is the story of anyone who has ever taken a chance on a new city or a new life.

But there is so much here that is unique as well, and the details of that unique life are rendered beautifully, poetically. "The Inferno" is easily one of the best pieces of creative non-fiction I've come across in recent memory, and the fluid, graceful movement of images in "The Journey" is a clear indication that something very special is happening in these pages.

In the end, we are enriched, and become convinced that technology and art can be – and perhaps already are -- one and the same. We are also left with the mark of an outstanding writer: we leave this book wanting more.

Will Curl, Ph.D.

Lecturer in English, University of Wisconsin – Fox Valley.

WHERE IT ALL BEGAN.

...THE BIRTH OF
ARTIFICIAL
IMAGINATION

Into the Heart of the Mind

Does the mind have a heart? Does the heart have a mind? Is it a pain to have a mindless heart, or a heartless mind? What if you have to have both?

University of California, Davis, photo by Kalpanik S.

The story begins in the computer center of a 20th century American university in 1987. It's a warm October afternoon. Birds are chirping, flowers are blooming, a breeze is blowing, and Americans are driving their Japanese automobiles: in short, everything is going on as it should.

Is it really? Looking closer at the computer center, we see a maiden with a melancholy look on her face. She is staring blankly at the screen in front of her. It is already Thursday. The homework is due tomorrow.

She has to write a computer program for matrix inversion using the Gauss Elimination method. She does not really care a bit whether matrices have any desire to be inverted, let alone their preference for an algorithm for inversion.

In fact, all this Wildlife and Fisheries Biology senior is interested in thinking about is her weekend skiing trip. But she has to pay the price for having a desire to finish her college degree. The university requires every student to do a basic programming class, and she was so terrified of doing it that she postponed it until her last year in school.

The time is ripe for our hero to walk onto our stage: the computer center. He is an essential part of the American engineering education system, the foreign born Teaching Assistant.

The girl very coyly asks him for help. He is all for it. He has started on his mission to make the world a better place by banishing human pain and suffering. The sight of a damsel in distress, a pretty girl struggling with matrices, melts his heart. He forgets all of his own troubles...

His troubles? Yes; he is already regretting what he did exactly a year ago. Instead of spending a Saturday playing cricket, driving his Vespa up and down New Delhi roads or daydreaming, he spent it darkening circles on a piece of paper with a pencil. After trying his best at creating a masterpiece for three hours, he handed over his artwork to eager hands and walked out of the scene and forgot all about it.

But the misdeed had been done. The piece of paper was mistaken for an answer sheet for the Graduate Record Examinations and flown to GRE, Princeton, NJ, USA. American optical scanners and computers pounced on it, processed it and, after brooding over it for a while, came up with their decree -- the poor chap

was assigned a 3-tuple of bounded positive integers--
(***,***,***) which sealed his fate.

After that, everything happened in an instant. Less than
a year later, he was exiled to the USA for at least two
years. If his conduct was good during the exile, he
would be awarded a Master's degree at the end of it.
They agreed to cover his living expenses during his exile
through a combination of a fellowship and a TAship.

He also had a choice of location: he could either fly east
from New Delhi to the West coast or fly west to the
East coast.

After accepting the hardship of fate, he chose the
lesser evil of the two—west. The climate is warmer,
and California has both Silicon Valley and Hollywood in
it. So even if he failed to make it big in Silicon Valley
earning megabucks designing computers, he could give
the dreamland a second try on the silver screen.

He attends a cultural adjustment course offered by the
American Embassy. They use the term "cultural shock"
to describe the adjustments a foreign student needs to

go through in the US. A "shock"? Come on, it won't be that bad!

In that training, he is informed of the rather interesting fact that Americans smile a lot more than other cultures. However, unlike other cultures, the smile is a greeting, more of just a casual facial expression. It is not meant to be an invitation or a sign of intimacy.

Wise, all-knowing elders, who have never ever been outside the country, still don't hesitate from giving him their valuable advice -- he should focus on his studies, and not fall for the worldly temptations the western world is infamous for. And he should pay no attention to girls, girls in US are like butterflies, and have a new boyfriend every week!

The moment of parting arrives: our hero says goodbye and makes a dive over the Pacific Ocean to arrive in the land of opportunity.

Kalpanik Jumps Over a Lagoon in Santa Barbara, California.
Photo by Raja.

So he has arrived in the land of his dreams! California,
United States of America! That is where they make
those chips, not potato chips you silly, the
semiconductor chips, the microprocessors, the
computers, and write all that software. The land of
Intel, Apple, IBM, DEC and Microsoft!!

He is shocked by how pale their faces look; somehow
the color from their faces (and in some cases, their
hair) has bleached out.

They all speak English with such a heavy "foreign" accent. And the food! How different is their food. Whatever vegetarian stuff they serve is raw or undercooked and is so bland, so tasteless. No spices. Ugh.

Before he knows what's really happening, he is standing on the wrong side of the class with a bunch of rough and tough kids giving him a nasty look. Those who do not qualify as rough and tough -- primarily because they don't belong to the rough & tough gender, gaze at him with horror in their eyes, as if he was telling them ghost stories or dirty jokes!

Can they not understand what he is saying because of his accent? He is already getting used to theirs. Or was his younger brother's opinion, that he is absolutely incapable of teaching, correct?

Well, life isn't handed over to everyone on a silver platter. Here's the deal, take it or leave it.

Let's return to our original scene, the one with the melancholy maiden, the damsel in distress. The teacher starts teaching, the student starts learning and the matrices start getting inverted.

Two hours later, all the matrices in the world that were supposed to be inverted have faithfully done so. Our hero is satisfied. His younger brother was wrong after all. He can teach. Also, humanity overall is happier than it was 2 hours ago.

Gosh! We haven't given a name to our characters yet. Since he claims to be a mathematician at heart, let's call him "X". No, X has to be used for the other variable in the equation, because that has appeared first. Let's call him "Y".

The Earth rotates around its axis a few more times as per its old, bad habit of doing the same thing over and over again.

Y is going through the biggest transition a human being can undergo.

Not only has he traveled between two places which are at the greatest possible distance from each other, he has also time-traveled 40 years into the future, into a world of coin-operated machinery and coin-operated human beings, a world richer in materialistic wealth but arguably much poorer otherwise.

Culture Shock? Yep, those Embassy folks weren't lying.

Women don't wear pretty colorful saris but wear ugly looking blue jeans. Students can afford cars, but need to clean their own bathrooms, cook their own meals, wash their own clothes. In Delhi, there were maids to do all this. Most students bring cold sandwiches for lunch to save money. Where else in the world do people eat cold food for lunch? He can't!

Switches are on from down to up. Traffic follows the right lane.

The laws of nature are cruel: struggle for existence, survival of the fittest.

Y struggles. He adapts. Is he fit enough to survive?

He is getting used to the new daily routine. He attends classes in morning, assists his students with their assignments in the afternoon, and finishes the day by doing homework with his Malaysian Chinese classmate. They carry out a comparative analysis between the various spiritual, intellectual and emotional aspects of Chinese, Indian and American girls.

He eats dinner with his Mexican roommate, who is studying killer bees' migration patterns to prepare for their arrival in Mexico. They drink Kahlua together, his first alcoholic drink.

Time to go to bed. He feels restless and can't go to sleep. He is missing something in his life. What? What??

Life as a Teaching Assistant (TA) is sort of interesting, especially if you have to be in the computer center at the peak time, the day before the submission deadline.

One is in great demand. It makes you feel that you are wanted; the world is not complete without you.

You can get carried away and end up spending twice as much time with your students as you are allocated, if you like getting the attention.

And if you are a Teaching Assistant in an engineering department in an American university, you also get to meet people from all over the world.

You get to explain the nested DO loops to Jordanian hydraulics Engineer Bali Khaled, and learn about the weird politics of the Middle East.

Talk in Urdu to the Pakistani applied physics major Mohamad, clarifying the IF-THEN-ELSE condition. Did you know Urdu is really the same as Hindi!

Teach the computer editor commands to Jin Ping, from mainland China.

Work with Apollo, the American mechanical Engineering student, to get rid of the mysterious UNIX bus error. Apollo is such a smart kid. He'll make a good Engineer!

Help out Barbara, the girl with such a quizzical look on her face, with subroutine calling and parameter passing. He likes her as a teacher likes a good student.

Point out the error in declaration of variable type to Krysten– this Vietnamese girl is tiny and very delicate looking, but she picks up stuff really fast.

Calm down nervous Brenda -- all computer programs ultimately run, though most of them only run at 5 PM on Friday just before the time of submission. When her boyfriend comes to pick her up Friday evenings and can't really do anything to help her out except call the Indian TA, well, the look of jealousy on his face is worth a million dollars.

And finally there is X, the girl in the second paragraph of our story. The girl with a shy smile.

The story of the second, 6th and 14th paragraphs is repeated every week The matrix inversion is replaced by matrix functions, file manipulation, differential equations and all the other stuff which engineering professors consider necessary to teach their students.

Of course Y's assistance is required. He assists her in writing and debugging her computer programs.

Besides many other undesirable tendencies, human beings have a particularly silly one. They like to know about each other and talk about themselves whenever they can. Some actually do so to their pets, which classifies as cruelty to animals.

So while the computer is busy compiling and running her program, being human beings, they talk.

She does not like asking him for help. It hurts her sense of achievement. Even he does not like asking others to help him out, but sometimes it is necessary.

Is he a Ph.D. student?

No, he is doing his Masters in Computer Engineering. Yes, being a TA helps with the college expenses. He doesn't really mind doing it though. He likes teaching things he knows to others.

Her brother is turning more human. Her sister just got married. Her parents are visiting Europe. She went to Australia to study for a year. She likes playing, skiing, dancing and all outdoor activities. She is not all that enthusiastic about studies though.

He has just arrived in the US. He likes their nation; but does not think it is a great idea to welcome foreigners by sending them telephone bills for 300 dollars. He makes just 900 dollars a month after taxes. One day, he will write programs for AT&T and leave a few bugs in it.

To make it worse, someone stole his bike.

She just broke up with her boyfriend, since he was cheating on her. She's not looking for a relationship anymore, but wants to focus on her studies this year so that she can graduate.

Relationship? What an unromantic term to describe deep human feelings between two people. Wow! Aldous Huxley was right! In the Brave New World, people don't fall in love any more, they get into relationships!

No, he doesn't see himself ever having a "relationship" with anyone, though it is very likely he will fall in love with someone at the right time in the right place.

Is every student as silly as she is?

No, he does not find her silly. OK, just a little bit silly.

He said that on purpose to make her blush. He likes watching her blush.

Does he go home every summer?

All the previous 21 summers, he was in India.

Is he only 21 and doing his masters? She blushes again; she is 23, older than him, and still trying to finish her Bachelors. He must be really smart.

No news there, yes, he is.

She does not look that old; she looks more like 18.

He likes her. This time, his affection for her may not be totally classifiable as a teacher's affection for his student.

Is it unethical for him to feel affection for her?

She is older than he is and she seems to be smiling a lot to him. But he remembers the "culture shock" lesson he was taught at the embassy. In their culture, the smile is just a greeting, an encouragement, maybe a sign of sympathy. It is not meant to be an invitation or a sign of intimacy.

Strangely, neither of those two facts stops his heart from practicing Michael Jackson beats every single time he sees her smile.

Well, Y is not here only to teach and meet other people from the globe. He is supposed to study and do research.

Research isn't as easy as it used to be 100 years ago. Then all one had to do was to sit under a tree, watch an apple fall, scratch one's head and write a couple of differential equations and BINGO, the world gets Newton's mechanics.

In the 20th century, research involves reading thousands of research papers and attending hundreds of research conferences just to keep track of what other smart guys are up to. After that you have to carry out computer simulations until you get sick.

Then, if you are lucky enough, you can find a smart way which will reduce something somewhere by 0.2%. But then what? You have to collect a bunch of lunatics like yourself who can understand the technical details of your stuff and tell them how smart you are!

But still, doing research has its own rewards. It's like giving birth to a baby. It's a painful and laborious process, but one ends up with a joy of creation and a sense of achievement.

But before doing any research, you have to decide your area. Y's playground is Electronics and Computer Technology.

Electronics and Computer Technology, the world of black magic. Rip apart an electronic system and you see nothing moving, nothing vibrating, in fact you don't see much at all. It's almost a make-believe world, a child's fantasy, a writer's imagination. The only thing that makes you believe in it is that it works.

A field which moves so fast that it outdates itself every year. A field that has revolutionized the way human beings live, think and act. It makes all the brains in the world get together in the land where they build those dream machines.

University of California, Davis. Photo by Kalpanik S.

It's also an area that involves billions and billions of dollars in terms of money. Yes, money. The corporate giants -- IBM, Apple, DEC, INTEL, Oracle, Microsoft -- are willing to pay a lot of it to every good technical resource they can get, no matter where he or she was born!

Money, which makes little kids leave their nice, cozy homes and go to another land to live among strangers.

Electronics and Computers. It is wonderful. It is exciting. It is glamorous. It is full of youthful energy. It has a lot of money in it, but it requires heartless minds, it has no place for emotions. It requires giving up your life as you knew it and going far away from home.

Before doing any research, Y has to learn some tricks already known in the field by doing graduate level courses.

What does doing graduate level courses mean?

To begin with, you go to classes and nod your head a few times to convince your professors that their attempts at teaching are not fruitless, avoid being caught while taking a nap and daydream with your eyes open.

Afterwards, sometime when the rest of humanity is doing what humanity normally does in the middle of night, you have to make some sense out of the nonsense. This requires reading.

Let's start with the section on Error Detecting Codes and Self Checking Circuits in his book on Fault Tolerant Computers. The world needs its computer systems to be fault tolerant so that they can reliably process transactions 24 hours a day, seven days a week.

It talks about vector subspaces in the binary Galois field and further goes on to derive ten (10) properties of the unsystematic Hamming codes.

Now, vector subspaces in the binary Galois field is not exactly a piece of cake, but you still can't intimidate Y with it. He is paid a scholarship just because he can make sense out of the nonsense, and he does exactly that.

Then he goes on to next section. It says that unfortunately, the linear system model developed in the last section is not sophisticated enough to deal with cyclic codes. So it introduces polynomial algebra with arithmetic module X^n+1.

Now, isn't that pushing the matter too far? I mean, why be greedy? Why not just manage with what you can get out of vector subspaces in the binary Galois fields?

Three hours and two cups of tea later, he figures it all out. He feels so much more knowledgeable.

Now, let's read about the next subject. He starts reading a research paper for his Advanced Computer Architecture course, written by a very smart chap from IBM research labs, Yorkshire Town Heights, New York. The first paragraph mentions the phrase "advanced computing" three times and he likes it instantaneously.

He goes on to read the second paragraph. It says if you do something to something mentioned in the first paragraph, then something becomes more efficient by 30%. A full thirty percent improvement? Wow! What a smart chap! He must have a lot of gray cells.

Now the third paragraph. But wait a minute. He hasn't really understood what exactly has been going on. Back to first paragraph. Repeat until it makes sense.

Done.

And now, a field he really likes, Artificial Intelligence. Create a computer that can not only think, but can also reason, learn, remember and understand language, and use those abilities to play chess, give expert advice and talk to patients about their symptoms and cure them.

Can this be done? Isn't this playing God? And if we created thinking machines that could think better than us, what would we do?

And won't it be more fun if we could write programs which could imagine like humans, and simulate feelings, creativity and even humor? Yeah, build a computer which was really funny!! Computers that could laugh and cry, fall in love, had ambitions and aspirations, hopes and fears, dreams and nightmares. Computers that became sad if their users did not appreciate them, that became jealous if their owners looked at other, shinier computers.

OK, he was wildly imagining again. Or maybe Artificial Imagination was possible, but the time wasn't right; maybe he needs to wait for a few years before talking about computers that could laugh and cry, pick an argument over the internet, believe and reboot for those beliefs.

First he needs to learn about Artificial Intelligence, finish his assignments for Prolog.

Prolog is a programming language which allows programmers to build rules which can be used to build a knowledge base, an expert system. The expert system can simulate human expertise based on these rules, which can capture years of knowledge gained by an expert.

They studied the "Cut" predicate today, but he didn't really get it. He needs to read about it again.

But it's 4 AM! He has a class at 8, in another four hours!

Maybe he should've spent less time with his students, and gone home at the end of the allocated time, rather than staying with them in the lab. But he likes them, he enjoys the big brotherly feeling.

Maybe he should stop reading books other than his textbooks -- humor by P.G. Wodehouse, sociology by Alvin Toffler, literature by Somerset Maugham and Orwell, and sensational thrillers by Ludlum. Or maybe stop riding his bike along those beautiful green fields wondering about the origin of the Cosmos.

Wait a second. He has never forced himself to study before. He always balanced his studies with other activities. Dropping everything else will be equivalent to sacrificing his life for a career in Hi-Tech. Hasn't he already sacrificed enough? Maybe it's time for deciding priorities.

Priorities? Didn't he set his priorities when he left his home for US? His life is now Electronics and Computer Technology -- it is his hopes and fears, his dreams and nightmare his laughs and tears, and his best friend and worst enemy.

Life is Full of Twists and Turns, Photo by Kalpanik S.

He has travelled 8000 miles for the famed Silicon Valley, and he is so close, only 80 miles away from it! This is only a weak moment; it should go; damn it, it has to go.

And this is no longer just about him anymore. He remembers the demographics of his Fault Tolerant computer design class.

Four American born students sit on one side of the class and the other side is taken by the rest of the "world": one Taiwanese, one mainland Chinese, one Korean, one German, one Malaysian, and him, the only Indian. As the sole representative of his country, he can't just give it up.

Maybe the answer is in his book? Let's see what it says -- Chapter 4:

"The Prolog cut predicate, or '!', eliminates choices in a Prolog derivation tree. If you get to the cut, it always succeeds and the derivation tree is trimmed of all other choices to the point where the cut was introduced into the sequence of goals.

So in simple words, reaching a '!' in the sequence of clauses implies that **if you get this far, you have picked the correct rule for your goal.**

Since all the remaining alternative choices between the parent goal and the cut have been discarded; reaching a cut also means that **if you get to here, you should stop trying to re-satisfy your goal."**

Isn't there a deeper meaning hidden in this description of the cut clause? Let's read it again.

If you get this far, you have picked the correct rule for your goal?

If you get to here, you should stop trying to re-satisfy your goal?

Yes, there was! Suddenly, everything became crystal clear:

If you get this far, you have picked the correct rule for your goal!

If you get to here, you should stop trying to re-satisfy your goal!!

The moment of weakness is over.

The architect who designed the human "computer" created two models of the same machine with a slight difference in their firmware: One model of the species had the second chromosome of the 23rd pair as X, the other as Y.

The whole idea seems to be to make the system run efficiently and smoothly, all by itself; while the creator just sits by the side and watches the game with amusement, sipping his beer and smoking his cigar.

X and Y: the coding scheme stinks. It creates a mess, especially during tough times and weak moments. The times when a show of sympathy can mean a lot to the kid who is trying to show the world that he is an adult, a go-getter, a winner. Times when being told that he is smart does him wonders, times when a smile can mean a lot.

X & Y–let's return to our characters with those strange mathematical names.

Some sort of a relationship is developing between the teacher and the student.

She smiles at him so sweetly. Is it just womanly sympathy? Is she just being nice and friendly to the lonely foreigner? He likes her smile. But then, in this culture, the smile is supposed to be just a greeting, a sign of encouragement or sympathy. It is not meant to be an invitation, does not indicate any intimacy.

Downtown Davis, Photo by Kalpanik S.

How can someone smile so sweetly and not mean anything?

She does say "Don't leave me alone" in a flirtatious way when his allocated lab time is over and he tries to leave; she is not finished with her assignment yet.

But then, those are just words. And in the US, women flirt; it doesn't really mean anything. She just needs him to help her finish her assignment. Even then, he stays back an extra couple of hours to help her debug her programs. What a romantic way to spend an evening.

And yes, there are still other students who need his help. And yes, he likes helping them all, especially Apollo and Krysten, they are the smartest among them. But he does not think about them as much after the lab as he thinks of X.

Has he found an oasis in the desert?

Later, in the library, Y cannot control himself and looks up an article on love by the French author F. S. Croulant:

"Love is a little nearsighted, maybe, but not blind. The male animal is not necessary looking for a looker. The list of qualities men seek are openness, honesty, understanding, physical attractiveness and intelligence. Men also want someone who respects them and someone with whom they feel comfortable.

Biochemists say in love, the mere sight of a face or sound of a voice causes the glands to release a number of hormones into the body and set off a lightning-like chain reaction affecting the entire system. Blood pressure rises. The pulse quickens. Circulation races. The face blushes. The pores of the skin open and beads of perspiration appear."

(The heart starts practicing the latest Michael Jackson beats.)

"Love is an ideal vehicle for addiction because it can ideally claim a person's consciousness. When continuous exposure to something is necessary to make life bearable, an addiction is established."

The addiction has been established.

Unfortunately, the continuous exposure is a job requirement. His professional duties include spending several

hours with her every week helping her out. She does need his help. Computer programming is tough for non-Engineering students.

Computer terminals, especially if two people work on one, can bring people closer.

Physical proximity. Emotional Intimacy.

Need. Emotions. Desire. Craving?

That unexplainable feeling of just wanting to be with someone.

X and Y - the coding scheme stinks.

The quarter ends. The exam for E-5, basic programming class is over. The worker comes to collect the examination answer sheets. He will spend the next week grading these.

They meet.

She greets him, with her usual sweet smile. She knows that he likes her smile, and she bestows it generously upon him. He does not ask her the question.

He can't; remember, he is the teacher. Even if she is older, richer and the native, that still does not change the rules.

She does not give him the answer. How can she, if he doesn't ask the question?

They part. She smiles one last time, a sweet smile. Maybe there is an answer in that smile. He just needs to decipher it.

OK kid, it was good knowing you, as one of my students, as my first time teaching experience. You were a tough student to teach, tougher than a younger brother. You are going to remain in my memory until it runs out of swap space.

Sentimental types, hold your tears, no need to cry now, the story hasn't ended. Yes, there is more to come.

The reviews for Teaching Assistants are in. He is curious, but also nervous. How did he do as a TA, how had his students rated him? Isn't it strange that his first ever job turned out to be teaching students in a foreign country, in his third language?

"I enjoy the informal format of the discussions." Ha! They like his jokes, jokes they could only half understand. His younger brother was definitely wrong: not only can he teach, he turned out to be a good teacher.

Wait, it gets even better!

...y is a good TA, he helped me a lot on debugging most of my programs. Furthermore, he gives good example in the discussion on some of the programs that are related to homework

His students like him! Even though he has an accent, the Americans like him! He has succeeded in his first job! His hard work, all those extra hours have paid off!

This also helps him heal from a case of a bad grade, a B given by the Professor who had taught the class on Artificial Intelligence.

As his term assignment, Y had presented the concept of Artificial Imagination to the class, a computer program which could simulate human creativity, imagination and humor, and presented a sketch, a blueprint to the class on how such a program could be built.

The class laughed through it, but the Professor thought that Y was being frivolous, and handed him a B!

But with the spectacular review feedback in his hand Y tries to forget about X and about the sore feelings from the getting the B, and goes out with his Austrian and Brazilian friends to carry out research work about the electrifying effects of the night life of Las Vegas, the fun capital of the world. Unfortunately, their research project had to be stopped in the middle because of lack of funding.

You have a dirty mind, don't you? Otherwise, what made you think what you're thinking?

He comes back and sees a note in his mailbox from Judy, his department's administrative assistant. He goes to see her. She gives him a sly smile and tells him that two girls have left packets for him.

What packets? And girls? !@*&?? Two girls? The first
one is a packet of cookies with a note of thanks from
Krysten, his smart, delicate Vietnamese student:

> ·Y
>
> Thanks for all your
> help with my programs!
> Couldn't have done them
> without your patience!
> You're an awesome TA!
> Keep up the good work.
> Have a great vacation &
> Merry Christmas! ☺
>   Krysten
>   Nguyen

Did you read it? Read it again! How nice of her! And he
didn't really spend that much time with her; she's
smart.

This proves once again that he did well in his first job,
in another country, speaking his third language. He
feels about ten feet tall.

This proves another point. Women, irrespective of being Indian, East Asian or Caucasian, irrespective of being short or tall, irrespective of the fact that they can operate heavy machinery and program computers in the 20th century, still absolutely reserve their right to feed men from time to time. Otherwise, why didn't any of the male students think of baking cookies for him ;-), eh?

What's in the other packet? Judy had said two girls, so this is from the other girl. What other girl? His heart starts practicing Michael Jackson beats again.

Cookies again! This one is from X.

The two cookies on the top of the box are in the shape of a heart. Colored red, with red sugar.

Hmmm, so the smile was more than just a greeting, and a casual facial expression. Otherwise why the heart shape, the red color, why two of them? Isn't that supposed to be an invitation?

There is no note though, no phone number.

There is only one way to know for sure. He needs to ask, otherwise he will never know; never know for sure. He will always have a doubt.

Should he call her? No, that would not be romantic. He should probably write to her.

How about this for a draft?

Hi X,

Thanks a lot for those really delicious cookies. That was really nice of you. It gave a boost to my "sense of achievement." Also, it is great to know that I have made friends on this side of the globe.

It would be nice to have friends who I could call without later receiving an intimidating letter from AT&T to pay a huge sum of money by a certain date or else face the dire consequences. And all this time I used to think that the USA had organized crime only in places like Chicago or New York!

I am going to miss you in Surge IV this quarter, especially Friday afternoons. A week of vacation in

Vegas could not root out the addiction acquired during last 10 weeks.

You have been a pretty good friend and I hope that the end of the professional relationship between us will not be the end of our friendship.

I am also enclosing an evaluation form modeled around the TA survey, I would appreciate it if you can fill it and send it back.

With warm regards,

Y

Letter Writing Evaluation Form:

Please evaluate Y on the items below using a UCD general purpose Answer Card and these categories:

A: Strongly Agree B: Agree C: Mixed Feelings D: Disagree E: Strongly Disagree N: No Opinion

1. Y's letters are well organized.

2. Y shows originality and creativity in his letters.

3. His letter makes interesting reading. (mark N if you've never read his letters)

4. Y shows enthusiasm for the subject matter.

5. Y has got a sense of humor.

6. It is clear in his letters what he means.

7. Overall Y is a good letter writer.

Please write comments, if any, at the back.

This sounds humorous but sincere. She may or may not like him, but she has to be amused by this.

Now the tough question -- should he send it?

Come on kid, come to your senses. Note the tremendous differences: the cultural, ethnic, social, national, racial, economical, lingual differences between the two of you.

You don't stand a chance. You are too different from her. And remember, you are here to pursue your academic and career ambitions, not to chase girls. You need to have a heartless mind.

On the other hand, unless he asks, he will never know. Can he live with that?

Why should he take the risk?

All the cultures around the world require a man to take the risk of asking, and the risk of rejection. He is a man now, isn't he? He has made it to the most advanced nation in the world, and they are paying him to be there. Yes, that definitely makes him a man.

The statistician calculates the probabilities. It is low, but non-zero. But the risk is too high; if he is rejected, he will always doubt whether it was because of his race.

Should he or shouldn't he?

To be, or not to be, that is the eternal question.

X had been waiting eagerly for Y to call. She had a crush on Y. He was tall, dark and handsome. She liked his jokes, his sense of humor. She liked his old-fashioned way of thinking, the way he talked about falling in love, and not having relationships. He was so romantic. He was completely different from any of the boys she had known.

She had been giving him hints all this time, she had smiled so sweetly at him, but he had not responded. What was stopping him?

Was it because she was older than he was? Or was it because she was not cute enough? She watches herself in the mirror. Her previous boyfriend had left her for someone else, after all.

Or did he misunderstand her "Wildlife and Fisheries" major as many others had? It was not about studying the wild lives of young college students, but about life in wilderness, about animals and fishes. No, not party animals, real animals! Animals living in the natural wilderness.

She could not be any more direct, could she? She even flirted with him, saying "Don't leave me alone" at the end of so many evenings.

Anyone else would have guessed her interest. He sometimes seemed interested but at other times, distant and afraid. Afraid of what?

She had finally gathered enough courage to send him those cookies in the shape of the heart, sprinkling them generously with red color. That was a very clear signal. He's supposed to be smart.

The fact that he didn't call means he isn't interested. She feels so bad about taking that chance, sending those cookies.

She cannot do anything more. She cannot take the risk of getting hurt again, by confessing her love to him. She has been hurt too many times.

Y read his letter again and again. It was funny. It was the most creative thing he had ever written. But he could not take the risk. The stakes were too high, the probability of success was too low.

Cupid had arranged everything right. They were brought together from two different worlds, thousands of miles apart, at the beautiful town of Davis in California. They both wanted each other, needed each other.

But it was not meant to be. He could not gather courage to respond to her inviting smile or her love message encrypted in those cookies.

She could not do anything more beyond what she already did.

So? With teary eyes, he throws the letter away. This was not home. And something hardens inside, into steel.

The metamorphosis is complete. The 21-year-old kid finally becomes a man: away from home, among strangers. X was the catalyst needed to complete the annealing process.

Now what?

Fasten your seat belt, push down the pedal, begin your journey! No time to stop or slow down, you have a long way to go.

Conquer this land. Conquer their minds, but more importantly, Conquer their hearts. Win their smiles.

Welcome to the United States of America!

The story begins . . .

The_PrOgrEM

```
                    PrOgrEM

10     It is the middle of the night,
20         we are alone together;
30     hopelessly in love,
40         we don't need to talk,
50     we just look at each other
60
70     surrounded by a low clattering sound
80         breaking the stillness of the night;
90     a few greenish lights blink around us,
100        a very romantic sight
110
120    I look at her shining face,
130        what is that bright look telling me?
140    Is it naughtiness my love,
150        or are you feeling shy?
160    hesitating, yet she is prompting me
170
180    I tap on her delicate body
190        Her face glows up bright;
200    She softly moans and complains,
210        I am not doing it right
220
230    Sometimes we talk all night,
240        Sometimes we even fight;
250    But she always tells me what's wrong;
260        and together we set it right
270
280    We form a perfect couple,
290        man and his machine,
300    programmer and his progem.█
```

13 years later

A Beautiful Voice

From: Me
Sent: Monday, June 15, 2002, 11:30 PM
To: My Friends
Subject: A Beautiful Voice

Friends,

I would not have thought that I would ever find anything—not even a woman's voice—beautiful at 5 a.m. As most of you know, I am not a morning person.

But when Conita called me at 5 a.m. today to inform me that the 1,500-foot geofence around my car had been violated, I found her voice so beautiful, so reassuring, so full of love, care, and hope that it almost brought tears to my eyes.

Now, being the techies that you are, instead of being caught in the sentimental spirit, and without even blinking an eye, you must be asking, what the heck is a 1,500-foot geofence? And isn't a voice supposed to be "sweet" instead of being "beautiful"?

But what you should really be asking me is why a woman would call me so early in the morning and what did she say that almost made me cry?

Sigh. You are all hopelessly unromantic.

Here are the technical answers: A geofence is a designated perimeter, a virtual circle, that you can draw around a movable object or body, such as your car (or your pet, or an elderly parent, or a precious asset), using Televoke or a similar system, to set the limits or boundaries of their expected movement—like a virtual leash. If the body or object (such as your car or pet) moves outside this perimeter, a notification is triggered that can be sent to you as a voicemail, a page, or an e-mail.

This neat trick is done using an electronic device that contains:

- an embedded GPS module that can detect its location by talking to three or more satellites

- a microprocessor which compares the object's current location with the stored center and computes if it has exceeded the set perimeter
- a wireless component that sends a packet to Televoke's network operations center when the violation happens

The Televoke system then queries the user preferences and notifies the user by calling, paging, or e-mailing him or her.

Geofencing is one of the many useful features that our system provides for automotive services by combining the power of GPS, wireless technology, automotive electronics, and plain old electric relays. (Relays are involved in opening door locks using your cellular phone—if you are locked out of your car, for instance.) This system can theoretically be extended to track and virtually fence pets straying from home, elderly people with memory loss, and small kids. We are waiting for the device sizes and current draw to come down.

Conita is our Voice User Interface/Speech Generation System, which is used for both inbound and outbound interactions such as notifying consumers or businesses when their car alarm goes off, their vehicle crashes, their son or daughter is driving too fast, or their employee takes the company-owned delivery van out of the expected delivery region. It is also used for the usual "press 1 for this, press 2 for that" prompt.

By the way, Conita's gender was decided long before I showed up here at Televoke. A customer service director I worked with at a dot-com once told me that most call centers use a woman's voice when they want the message or prompt to sound reassuring and caring. So don't flame me for stereotyping; I have no opinion on the matter.

Conita's call, which was triggered when my car violated the geofence set around it, was part of a test I had conducted. Her call meant that the system was working perfectly. Since many of you have released software, I don't need to explain the strong emotions we software pros get when we see our stuff working in production—it is the most beautiful, reassuring, and awesome thing in the whole world! It can bring tears of joy. (The non-software developers on this mailing list will just have to trust the rest of us on this.)

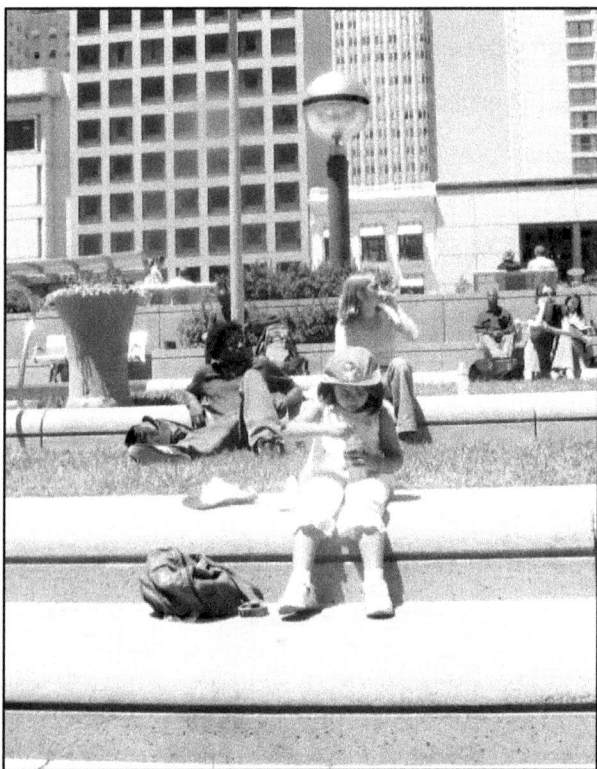

Union Square, San Francisco, California. Photo by Kalpanik S.

We released a new version of this software yesterday, June 14, 2002. My team implemented it in a live production environment last night. I was testing some of the old and new features early this morning, before our customers and our customers' customers wake up and use the new version.

A release day is always a big day for any software development group. At Televoke, it is literally a big day lasting 24 hours, and even more for a lot of people today (or was that yesterday?), after we worked through the last several weekends.

Now, unlike at Oracle or PeopleSoft where I could come in late the day after a release, I actually need to be here at 6 AM on such days. We run a 24/7 live ASP site, and the first thing our East Coast business customers do after they come to work the day after our release is to check out our website and our system, and call us with the few minor (really!) bug issues they find.

The day after a release, I also become the VP of Technical Support. That's usually a small part of my job, but it gets big the day after a release.

So how does a small 29-person startup provide 24/7 support with one tech support person? Well, the cell phone becomes the 24/7 support number. There's not enough head count, or even call volume, to have people working through shifts. And how does it feel to put my team through such a grueling work schedule? The same as it felt when I did it for my large employers: it sucks, but it's needed for the greater good of humanity.

If anything, asking them to give up their personal lives for the company's goals feels slightly worse now because I can no longer honestly claim that they are getting unusually valuable benefits (called stock options) compared to what they would get in other professions.

We want to change the world, though, and that is never easy. The world is usually very reluctant to change, especially at the pace startups want it to do so.

I thought this would be a beautiful way to tell you that I miss you all and to let you know what I really do for a living these days.

Me

Part Two:

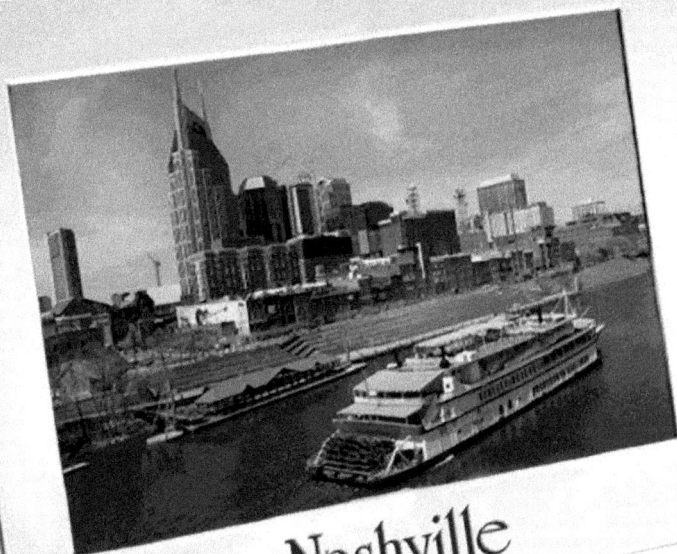

Nashville

The Journey

It is my first day at my new job in Nashville; I flew in from San Francisco yesterday. It has been snowing since the morning. I look through the office windows; I am fascinated by the soft, white, gorgeous carpet stretching for several miles in every direction.

The snowflakes descend slowly, floating in the air, allowing the current to carry them with it, letting it change their paths. They have chosen not to confront their destiny, choosing instead to enjoy every second of their short lives, their journey to the ground.

So how did I go from San Francisco, California to Nashville, Tennessee of all places? Here is the story.

After several months of marathon effort by me and other executives, our startup finally got acquired.

All of my "kids" kept their jobs, and the product we worked so hard to build will stay alive.

What about me? Well, after the merger, we ended up with two VPs of Technology, which was one too many. So I became part of the latest trend in the Hi-Tech world.

What trend am I talking about? If you live in the Silicon Valley, look around. What's hip these days among the Techies, especially the young executives of the boom days?

Silicon Valley, a Photo from Space

I'm talking about becoming unemployed, of course! While most of you wake up every morning and go to work worrying about keeping up with the many reasonable and unreasonable demands your bosses, peers, and customers make, we, the luckily unemployed, don't have to! We can sleep late, hang out in the real or cyber world until early morning and wake up at noon.

So like tens of thousands of others in the Tech industry, I took the dive. But before I could enjoy my unemployment, I had to take care of a couple of issues.

The first one was fixing my broken heart. I really loved my work and my team. I know, management is one of several professions where it is not considered a good business practice to get emotionally involved with your work. But I did. Don't they say it is better to love and lose than not to love at all?

I thought about it, and then bought a couple of tubes of Super Glue and a ticket to Las Vegas.

I worked diligently for next 36 hours at Harrah's, eventually ending up in their night club, surrounded by loud music and a few youngsters working very hard shaking their bodies in unimaginable ways. If I was still employed and had any open positions, I would have hired them for their creativity and hard work.

By 4 AM and after 2 drinks, served by a waitress whose interesting and innovative apparel would not be of much interest to any of you, I was finished gluing back all the broken pieces inside my heart.

Well, almost all; a few pieces were still missing. I suspect I left them behind at Televoke, PeopleSoft and Oracle Corporation.

So after taking care of the first issue, I moved on to the second.

This was what we VP-types refer to as having to come up with a communication strategy.

It is surprising how many people every day express their desire to know about your employment status in so many hideous ways. From the car mechanic to the optometrist to the young person with a sweet smile sharing the lunch table in a conference, everyone wanted to know some detail about my employment status: my work number, my employer's name or simply what I do.

In place of using the euphemistic "I'm between jobs," I chose to give the straightforward "I'm unemployed" as my reply. That usually spooked people, sometimes got me deep discounts, and usually resulted in a sympathetic smile.

Oh yeah, to that young person with a sweet smile, who was sharing my lunch table at a conference, to her I replied that I was searching for the meaning of life. She thought about it for a while and replied hopefully "Are you in bio-informatics?"

I decided to enjoy my unemployment by having other people pick up the tab for my travel to others parts of the USA, by pretending to interview with them. Silicon Valley, once known for having the highest density of millionaires per square mile, was now known for having the highest density of unemployed Techies per square mile. It was now a hunting ground for the recruiters from the rest of the country. My search for the meaning of life took me to sunny San Diego, musical Nashville and cold and icy Boston.

Just to make sure that these nice folks didn't end up hiring me, I interviewed in a leather jacket and black jeans. And I talked in an incomprehensible accent -- this one comes naturally to me.

Instead of answering their questions, I kept on bringing up a fairy tale in the interview, a tale of an ambitious young man who flew through heavens to a beautiful land, rescued a couple of damsels in distress and helped the emperor build his empire, the Emerald City.

During one of the interviews, after speaking passionately for a long time, I suddenly realized my audience had become very quiet.

I looked at the three interviewers; they were all silent, and had strange looks on their faces. Were they completely mesmerized by my powerful speech? Or did they not understand even a single word of what I said, because of my accent?

Either way, I ended up with an offer—a very good one, the position as the Head of Technology, managing sixty people! The company was profitable, and growing! And, sorry if it sounds like bragging, but, Umm, the job came with a large corner office. Finally!

But there was a catch. The job was in Nashville, Tennessee.

Say what? Nashville, Tennessee? Isn't that supposed to be a really bad place for an ethnic minority?

Well, here was the surprise. The company was owned primarily by a Chinese family. 40% of the Engineering group was born outside of USA and represented 5 different countries as their birth places.

Not only did the company fly both of us out for a visit to make up our minds, the CEO came to the airport to greet us personally!

Wow! So this is what the legendary southern hospitality means! I had been sought after many times before, but none of my suitors made such a personal gesture. I never felt so desired before! Being sought after always feels good; it felt more so in those times.

Still, move so far away? Leave my friends, my hometown, my favorite restaurants, the hiking and biking paths behind? For what? Just for my career?

And didn't I leave home once before? Isn't once enough for a lifetime?

Here's what an "expert," Alvin Toffler, has to say about this in his book Future Shock:

"We find an increasing number of technical populations are among the most mobile of all Americans. And we find an increasing number of affluent executives who move far and frequently . . . Among the people of the future, movement is a way of life, liberation from the constrictions of the past, a step into the still more affluent future."

I liked the sound of that. An "affluent executive" sure sounds like a pretty cool dude. I also liked the idea of being one of the "people of the future".

I looked at her; there were tears in her eyes. But she said yes.

It is my first day at my new job in Nashville. I look through the windows of my large corner office, and watch the snow fall.

The snowflakes descend slowly, floating in the air, allowing the air current to carry them with it, letting it change their direction. They have chosen not to confront their destiny, choosing instead to enjoy every second of their short lives, their journey to the ground.

I Met a Greek Goddess in Nashville

god·dess

n.

1. A female being of supernatural powers or attributes, believed in and worshiped by a people.
2. A woman of great beauty or grace.

It is Thursday evening in Fremont, California. My wife is back from her work. As the sun goes down, she starts feeling melancholy. I flew back to Nashville four days ago, and will not be back for another seven days. I had just accepted an offer in Nashville for a Senior Vice President position, and we had decided to wait till the school year was over before we moved our family.

She is missing me. Her eyes start filling up with tears. She realizes that she has been taking me for granted all these years, and recognizes the value I bring to the household, the gap I fill in her life.

You see, in our neighborhood in Fremont, you need to take the garbage containers out on Thursday nights for pick up early the next morning.

So how is Nashville?

Nashville is modern. The office building I work in is the most high-tech building I have ever worked in. It has live trees and fountains inside the building; Larry's emerald city had those outside. The security access to my office uses a fingerprint sensor, not the old fashioned badges most of you use in California! I couldn't guess the reason why the fingerprint sensor requires the finger to be warm, and didn't work when I didn't wear gloves on a cold day and my fingers were wet and cold (I haven't seen too many Bond movies lately). The 4-story high atrium has walls with 100% glass, and the rest of the building is 70% glass, reminding me of Larryland (Oracle Corp.). The result of an exterior of so much glass is large, XXXL sized windows.

Downtown Nashville, photo by Kalpanik S

I am ashamed to admit, that my office has, Umm, four of those extra large windows. Sorry, I don't want to be appear to be bragging, what can say-office space is perhaps cheaper in Nashville. But these windows do make me feel liberated, and one with the Universe. The view through those windows is simply spectacular; a view of "lovely, dark and deep" woods. Combine those woods with a few red brick buildings and an overcast sky, and I can finally see what inspired Robert Frost, who I quoted in the last sentence.

Robert who? Robert Frost was the 18th century English computer scientist who was famous for his white papers about the optimizing effects deep woods have on creativity programs running inside a human brain. Many say his research inspired Microsoft its campus among the deep woods in Redmond.

OK, so we have established that Nashville is beautiful. Now, is it a metropolis, or just a town?

What differentiates a city from a town? If I were a city, I would have felt very insecure in my citiness if I did not have a spectacular skyline, a maze of highways, and a population of at least a million folks. Nashville has all three: a population of 1.2 million, a maze of Highways 65/40/24 which almost matches the Bay Bridge/I-80 maze near San Francisco, and a spectacular skyline.

While it is a metropolitan, Nashville is simultaneously also like a 18th century European town.

It has a full size replica of the Parthenon, a Greek "temple" with a 42-foot-high sculpture of Athena, the

Greek goddess of wisdom, justifying being called the Athens of the South.

Is she a woman of exceptional beauty or grace, or a female being of supernatural powers or attributes?

To keep up with that Athens of the South image, there are a lot of buildings with brick or stone exteriors, very tall white pillars, and curved shapes. And I'm not just talking about old buildings; many of the new buildings have brick or stone exteriors too.

Parthenon, Nashville. Photo by Kalpanik S.

The brick buildings make Nashville a very romantic city; the view from the living room of my apartment includes the view of a curved building with tall white pillars, like sort of a Greek version of the Coliseum. The buildings in my neighborhood are genuinely old; they are part of Vanderbilt University. My neighborhood also has a few stone buildings, even homes. Maybe for these the stone is just on the outside. Oh yeah, there are many pretty trees as well around these spectacular buildings.

On the not so nice side, half of the city has the traffic lights hanging off of cables, rather than being on poles. My daughter noticed that right away on her trip here. On a bad day, a combination of those hanging traffic lights and the brick buildings looks creepy; but on most days, Nashville feels like a romantic, historic place.

So how is life for a minority in Nashville?

Let's start with the life of minority men. If you haven't heard, men are a minority in US; they form 49% of the US population, and 25% of the population of my household, with me representing the single male.

I have bad news for you, brothers. All those rumors about men receiving fairer treatment in the south are absolutely wrong. Discrimination against men is as rampant in Tennessee as in California. All the stressful, boring and inhumane jobs are done by men, like in California. This includes all the executive management jobs, and all the engineering jobs. It's no surprise that we die sooner!

The magazine covers here, like in California, have photographs of women, and that's true for men's magazines as well as magazines for women! What message are we sending to the next generation of men? That they will never grow up to be attractive enough to show up on a magazine cover? How will they get the self-confidence they so badly need to survive as a minority in their adult lives?

What about ethnic diversity in Nashville? How about my commute? What self-conscious remark did the counter girl at the Pancake Pantry make about being a Southerner? What's the strange thing about the Chinese restaurant in Brentwood? Read on...

Bridge over the Cumberland River, Nashville

Nashville, the Music City

Female Country Singer Playing Guitar, Nashville

Nashville is also known as the Music City, and indeed, Music is a big business in Nashville; making a whooping 6 billion dollars a year. all the recording studios like Warner Brothers, Sony, Columbia and many others have large offices here. More than half of all the single albums in the USA are published here. Many of the streets of the city are named after music: we have Music Circle, a Music Row, Music Square and Music Drive. No Music Parkway though.

And the music scene in Nashville includes more than just the country music. For example, my neighbor Faith Hill, who started her music career in country music, has gone beyond that genre and is now known as a pop singer.

When I informed my 11-year-old daughter over IM Messenger that Faith Hill lives in my neighborhood, she immediately did what 11-year-olds do: she pushed me a link to Faith's latest music video: "Cry".

The video, true to its name, depicts Faith, who is younger than me by less than a year, in tears.

Faith Hill album Cover from "Cry" , Photo reproduced under fair use
doctrine of United States Copyright Act

It has been known since ancient times that sight of a
damsel in distress, a woman in tears, incites strong
feelings of chivalry among men aged between 10 and
60. The male brain is somewhat weird in that regard.
Show us images of handsome, masculine men in tears
and we will turn our faces away in disgust! Show us a

helpless woman in tears, and we will try our best to help her.

A controversial study carried out at Stanford asserts that this strong feeling of chivalry gets further enhanced if the female subject under distress is completely drenched, like Faith is in the video. I completely disagree with the results of the study. I would have felt as strong a desire to help Faith out even if she was not drenched. After all, she is my neighbor, and like me, she has two young daughters.

Maybe she got drenched and is now crying because she forgot her umbrella at home? Maybe all I need to do is give her mine?

I decided to find out more about Faith's tears. My research over the web did not yield the reasons for her sorrow, but I found some very interesting similarities between us.

Both of us live in Franklin, Tennessee, have two daughters, have artistic talents and were born within a year of each other. Faith left home at age 19 to travel to another land to pursue her career ambitions; I did the same thing at age 21 (I traveled a lot farther though). She is a millionaire; I was a millionaire on paper once upon a time, but then the NASDAQ crashed, my stock options lost all their value and I became an ordinary person once again.

Both of us have web sites with photos of a pretty woman in them (www.faithhill.com, www.artificial-imagination.com). Faith has tens of millions of fans of her musical talent; I have thousands [Ok, may be just hundreds ☹] of fans of my writing talent.

There is one difference between the two of us: Faith does COunTRy music, I do COmpuTeR software.

This difference is not necessarily a bad thing: if Faith Hill was the Vice President of software development and came to the office drenched, the predominantly male software development staff would stop working and line up outside of her office in hopes of getting a glimpse of her.

On the other hand, I would probably not make a good country music singer. Have you ever heard of an Asian Indian country singer?

Not only there are no Asian Indians in the country music scene, there are no East Asians, African Americans or Latinos in it either. There is no equivalent of Beyonce, Jennifer Lopez, Coco Lee, Shakira or Ashanti in the world of Country Music, there is no diversity!

Thank Goddess, this lack of ethnic diversity in country music does not apply to Nashville as a whole.

Nashville is ethnically diverse. While it is not as diverse as California, where the non-Hispanic "whites" (the term used by US Census) are technically a minority (less than 50% of the population), it is still more diverse than Seattle. Nashville has 64% of its population as non-Hispanic whites.

Unlike the San Francisco Bay Area or the Northwest, the diversity in Nashville does not primarily come from Asians, it comes from African Americans. Also, the number of foreign-born citizens is much lower in Nashville. But then, where in the world would you have another place like Silicon Valley where 40% of the population is born outside the country?

While the number of Asian Indians in some Bay Area cities like Milpitas or Sunnyvale exceeds 10%, in Nashville, it is 0.5% which happens to exactly match the number of Asian Indians in Seattle.

What does that difference mean in practical terms? It means that in Milpitas or Sunnyvale, one out of every 10 persons on the streets, shopping centers and restaurants looks and talks like me; in Nashville, it's one out of 200.

Hence I stand out here. Fortunately, that's nothing new for me. I, Umm, always tend to stand out, right, friends? ;-)

People do ask me the question "Where are you from?" much more frequently here than they did in the SF Bay Area. My typical answer is: "Couldn't you tell by my accent? Most people are able to: I'm from California."

60% of the people get the joke and smile at my answer
(but still follow it up with "Where were you born?"),
while the rest don't understand my joke about my
accent because of my accent.

Southerners can sometimes be self-conscious of their
image of not being as progressive as other parts of the
country. For example, while paying at the counter at
Pancake Pantry, the cashier made a silly joke while
taking a look at me to match me with the photo on my
California Driver's license: "I really don't need to be
checking your photo, no one will ever try to
impersonate you because they won't be able to
pronounce their own name, he he he . . ." I gave her a
stern look. Her smile faded away and she added,
sheepishly, " . . . at least not us Southerners."

Also, not all of middle Tennessee is that diverse.
Brentwood, the suburb of Nashville where my office is
located, is more homogeneous than Nashville. This
means that at the Chinese restaurant in Brentwood,
the servers are Caucasians. I have been to Chinese
restaurants in far off places of the world, including

small towns in France, the Netherlands and Germany, but Brentwood is only the second place where I found a Chinese restaurant without Chinese servers.

My birth city, Delhi, is the first such place. Yes, India is much less diverse ethnically than any part of United States, though it is much more diverse in terms of languages, food, sub-cultures and religion.

Seattle

Inside the Giant Machine

I have been in Nashville for about a year. Unfortunately, the company I joined took a turn for the worse, and it was time to start my job search again.

Even though Nashville wasn't as bad a place for an immigrant family as many think, the work environment just wasn't the same as back in the west coast. So I decided to try to come back to the west coast.

One place and one company which I had looked at before had continued to haunt me over the year at Nashville, and were probably worth looking at again.

The place was Seattle, and the company, Amazon.

The Bizarre Bazaar

In 1993, Wall Street financial analyst Jeff Bezos and Seattle businessman Nicholas J. Hanauer were at a business lunch because they shared an interest in starting an Internet business. Hanauer wanted to invest in Bezos' idea for an internet bookstore and persuaded him to headquarter it in Seattle. Seattle was already a big IT location since Microsoft was located there (as well as Starbucks, Costco, and other big retailers.) And Seattle was close to the headquarters of the Ingram Book Group, the biggest book distributor in the U.S. at the time. When Bezos made the move in 1994, he had all his property shipped to Hanauer's home and set up "headquarters" in a Bellevue garage.

Why the name Amazon? Isn't that a river in South America? What's the connection with ecommerce? Bezos had originally picked "Cadabra", a short version of "abracadabra", the magical incantation that means, "To create as I say". However, "Cadabra" was too easily confused with the gruesome word "cadaver" and it appeared that it might lead to trademark issues with other companies using the name.

In the early days, internet directories such as Yahoo were still following the Yellow Book convention and were listing names of businesses alphabetically. Bezos wanted to make sure that his company would be listed at the top on any alphabetically sorted list so he wanted the name to start with "A". He methodically went through all of the A's in the dictionary and finally landed on "Amazon". The idea of "bigness" appealed to him. And perhaps, the fact that the word "Amazon" is also associated women warriors wasn't coincidental either and gave him a secret chuckle.

Working out of "headquarters" in the garage, Bezos and his handful of employees developed the software for Amazon.com, selling the first book in July 1995. The rest is, as they say, history.

Like the other modern entrepreneurial gods (Bill Gates, Microsoft and Steve Jobs, Apple), Bezos created Amazon in his own image. Who is Jeff Bezos? An article in *Fortune Magazine* painted this portrait of him: "Jeff

Bezos is having his picture taken jumping on a giant trampoline, and, remarkably, he looks like a man in his element. Most CEOs wouldn't pose for a photo like this in a million years. Risk life and limb to look undignified? Not a chance. But Bezos, who is 39, embraces the experience with the enthusiasm of a 10-year-old in an arcade."

Bezos' original business plan for Amazon, written during the drive from New York to Seattle, supported growth before profit, occasionally vexing his less visionary shareholders. In 2001, Amazon finally started showing signs of reaching profitability, posting a profit in the last quarter. Combined with its astounding growth, the signs were there that Amazon would soon become an unimaginably profitable company.

However, there were naysayers. Employees and former employees at Amazon revealed that top executives yelled at each other and their subordinates. Long hours were expected from all employees, and different groups were quite separated, with little top-down decision-making happening to bring teams together. Amazon paid very well and its corporate office hiring was very selective. However, employees reported a strong current of dissatisfaction within the company. Many employees found the corporate atmosphere at Amazon to be chaotic.

Amazon sent me what they call a "book bomb": three books on Seattle, Mike Daisey's "*21 Dog Years: Doing Time @ Amazon.com*", and James Marcus' "*Amazonia: Five Years at the Epicenter of the Dot.Com Juggernaut*". In his hilarious book *21 Dog Years : Doing Time @ Amazon.com*, Mike Daisey, a former Amazon employee who had joined the customer support group and then transferred to the business development department, portrayed the company as a falsehood, an unachievable dream, a company just pretending to be doing something great. He disclosed how he made up figures about his previous work in the customer service department when he was interviewing for transfer to the business development department. When he got the job, he congratulated himself on pulling a fast one; but later, upon reflection, he realized that the ability to make up good looking charts and numbers was the skill business development was looking for, not the ability to tell the truth. He said that at Amazon it did not matter whether the figures and charts you presented had any truth, what mattered at Amazon was that they looked good. Hmmm, that did not sound exciting. Fortunately, as I later found out, it wasn't really true—there is a lot of truth behind Amazon's image.

Daisey also said that Amazon sought out the "freaks" and with a major in aesthetics, he felt he fit right in. For some reason, that appealed to me. No, I wasn't a freak in the traditional meaning of the word; I did not have a Mohawk, or metal piercing or tattoos, but during my three-year tenure as an executive in Silicon Valley, I constantly felt that I did not exactly fit into the executive wing. To begin with, my "nerdiness", which can be expected of a computer-engineering graduate from the University of California, made me feel awkward in a suit and tie. In addition, I was also a foreigner, born and brought up in Delhi, India. I had brown skin and an accent; and somehow, despite the tremendous success of Indian and Chinese computer scientists in Silicon Valley, it was and is still rare for them to get into the top executive positions. Still, I felt that as an Asian Indian computer scientist with an odd accent and awkward manner, I might fit in with what Daisey called the "freaks" of Amazon. Indeed, he had joined Amazon for the same reason—he felt at home with the freaks.

Seattle is described as a medley of picturesque views of lush green hills surrounded by snowcapped mountains and sparkling blue waters. Seattle's mild winters and cool summers make the city lush and green. So true! If you visit Seattle in summer, you realize that Seattle in summer is the happiest place on earth. After living in a valley (yes, Silicon Valley really is a valley), I liked the idea of moving to a place surrounded by snowcapped mountains and sparkling blue waters.

I liked the idea for working a thirty-something CEO who defies his middle age by acting goofy like a kid. Bezos sincerely believed that his cult was changing the world and I wanted to be part of this revolution, and change the world!

Amazon, the world's largest e-commerce company, was transforming itself from an online retailer to a seller platform, an online bazaar (marketplace) where other merchants could sell their products.

So I decided to work for Amazon.

How to Get Hired by Amazon in Ten Days

Now of course, being hired by Amazon is not all that easy! No sir, you may have worked for more than a decade in Silicon Valley, but Amazon's young, sharp minds still want you to prove yourself to them. Hmmm, prove myself? I wasn't too sure about having to do that. Even though my master's project was about using a theorem-proving system, I thought my career success in Silicon Valley was all the proof anyone needed. But those were the rules so I took a deep sigh and got ready to prove myself, once again, in another land!

Still, despite all my brushing up on computer science basics, going over my work and defining my management strategy, I really wasn't prepared for the grueling interview process that followed at Amazon. It was a two-day-long marathon session that lasted 9 to 10 hours each day where 23 first-class prosecutors posing as interviewers grilled me extensively.

On their persistent insistence, I designed systems for real-time availability of inventory information, drop shipping, traffic light control, guaranteed message delivery, elevator controls, real-time availability of inventory (a second time), credit card authorization, email-based magazine subscriptions, distributed item management, top five reviews, a collaborative gifting system, and real-time availability of inventory (a third time—for some reason, they were really into real-time availability of inventory).

I came up with a data structure for snakes and ladders, a scheme for cache updating, and a scheme for storing binary trees in a relationship database management system (RDBMS).

I wrote a program to find a pair of numbers such that their sum is K, another to find the most frequent character in a list, a third one to find a string within a string within a string.

I estimated the computational complexity for programmatically resolving the inconsistency between various feelings incited by Ms. B. Spears among young fathers in their thirties[1].

I explained how Ms. J. Lopez's curvature could be described to a first order of approximation by using a hyperbolic paraboloid as a model (see diagram).

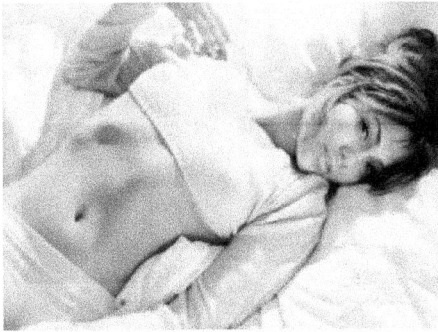

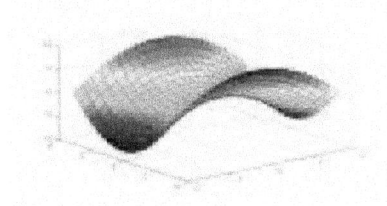

Ms. Lopez's curvature can be modeled using a hyperbolic paraboloid,
As depicted above

[1] George Michael, "Father Figure," Faith, Epic Records, 1987.

I predicted what happens if you put a print and a fork in a loop and stated how to determine the direction in which the stack grows programmatically.

I described object-relational mapping and the distributed transactions protocol.

I described my management style: how I assemble teams and motivate people, how I deliver projects on time with quality, how I let go of my employees and how I let go of my employers.

I described why my last dot-com failed, why my wireless startup succeeded, what keeps people at work late at night, and what keeps businesses prospering.

I explained J2EE, JSP, HTTP, TCP/IP, ISO 8583, ACH standards, hashing algorithms, B-trees, two-phased commit, DB normalization, serialization, horizontal partitioning and vertical segmentation, distributed architectures, and a database's ACID properties.

I came up with an innovative collaborative-gifting idea, suggested ideas for improving Amazon's website, explained web services, XML, SOAP, and my patent.

I solved several brainteasers, including the Monty Hall paradox, removing squares from grids, putting marbles in jars, and removing marbles from jars.

During one of the interviews, after speaking passionately for a long time, I suddenly realized my audience had become very quiet. I looked at the interviewers; they were silent and had strange looks on their faces. Were they completely mesmerized by my powerful speech? Or did they not understand even a single word of what I said, because of my accent? Either way, finally, I was allowed to go, all exhausted, after what seemed to be several weeks of grilling. In reality, it was only two days.

Two weeks later, I got a job offer from Amazon. Yay!

Except by this time, I also had another offer so I had to choose between the two. The other offer was better in financial terms, but Amazon had the promise of a revolution.

So was Amazon a real revolution? Or, as Daisey seemed to indicate, was it a made-up promise, never to achieve reality? I struggled with it for a whole week and then finally decided to turn down Amazon's offer. As I said before, the other offer was financially better and it seemed to have less risk of the unknown. Also, Amazon insisted on my signing a noncompete agreement, which said I could not work in a business that competes with Amazon for 3 years after leaving Amazon. Given that Amazon was getting into anything and everything, from ecommerce retailing to being a merchant platform to conducting online auctions to managing an online movie database, clearly, if they kept expanding at this rate it would mean that pretty soon I wouldn't be able to work for any internet company!

Amazon management was aghast. They could not believe that someone would give up an opportunity to be part of their organization. After all, they were the greatest thing on Earth!

After more discussion, we decided I would visit them and meet Rick Dalzell, Amazon's CIO. If I joined

Amazon, he would be my manager's manager's manager. On my request, they also agreed to fly in my wife and my daughters so they can check out Seattle. There was nothing to lose, in the worst case; we will have a family outing. Seattle looked like a beautiful place, but the two-day-long interviews hadn't left me any time to check it out. We stayed at W Seattle, an upgrade from the hotel I had stayed at during the interview.

Rick and I immediately clicked. To begin with, he came to meet me at a coffee shop next to my hotel rather than ask me to go to his office, making me feel like a VIP. Wow, a rare show of respect! He also had a lot of gray hair. I had recently developed a strong respect for people with gray hair, since I had gotten a few gray ones myself. And finally, like me, he had a plurality of daughters. Daughters are cool, and one is not enough. That established a common topic for conversation.

We compared notes on what age you have to start putting fences with live electricity around the house to keep all the boys out, where to get the GPS devices installed in the car when your daughters become eligible for a driving license, and how to write letters of protest to the CEOs of the teen fashion apparel companies. Ok, so I am kidding—mostly.

We discussed how Amazonians were able to balance their life with their work; most people worked less than 80 hours a week, and many worked only half day on Sundays. In fact, he was a taking a weeklong vacation this week even though he had taken one only five years ago. Even as we were speaking, his family was on board a cruise ship waiting for him. The ship was due to start its journey an hour ago, but the cruise company was holding it for him. After all, he was the CIO of Amazon, the world's largest ecommerce company. Why, if he wanted to he could buy the cruise ship, if not the cruise company, with his stock options.

His eyes glinted as he informed me that he would not be accessible by phone or email for the full week and that I was one of only 1,252 people to whom he was giving his personal hotmail account (to be used only in a true emergency).

Then, having proved beyond any shadow of a doubt that it was possible at Amazon to balance family life and work, we moved on to the financial aspects of the job. While he was not able to waive the non-compete agreement (he had to sign one too), he did make the deal sweeter.

Before I knew what was happening, my car was getting an 2500-mile ride on the back of a giant truck, and I was on a flight crossing the continent again – this time heading to Seattle, my eleventh work city.

Welcome to Seattle

Seattle's skyline at night. Photo by Dr. Colin Zheng

"Welcome to Seattle," the twenty-something car rental saleswoman said with a shy smile.

She looked both intelligent and pretty in her sleeveless top, glasses, and trendy low-rise jeans. Her shyness and apparent intellect reminded me of many of the female engineers I had worked with in Silicon Valley, but unlike them, she had a few delicate patterns tattooed on her upper arms. Then as she turned around, another tattoo peeked through the gap between her shirt and her dangerously low jeans. However, unlike the tattooed women I had seen earlier in San Francisco, who looked like biker women or high school dropouts, her tattoos were congruous with her shyness and air of intelligence. They added to her femininity, reminding me of my birth country, India, where women decorate their bodies with henna on special occasions. Over the next 24 hours in Seattle, I saw at least seven professional women with tattoos.

Now, my nondisclosure agreement (NDA) with Amazon does not allow me to reveal how many of the tattooed women I saw worked at Amazon. The only thing I am allowed to say is Amazon hires creative people who are independent in their thinking and are not afraid to express themselves.

But does Seattle really have a higher number of professional women with tattoos? Or was what I saw on my first day just a coincidence? My research on the web yielded these factoids:

- an article quoting Seattle tattoo parlors that the majority of their current clients are female college students or professionals

- a message thread on the Seattle Weekly's bulletin board, where "Date Girl" vigorously defends her stand that tattoos decorate a woman's body, not desecrate it

- an article saying that 22 percent of all Americans between the ages of 18 and 30 have tattoos

Say what? Twenty-two percent of my fellow citizens between the ages of 18 and 30 have tattoos? So all this time, I was living among this secret society of tattooed people? But if one-fourth of my fellow citizens have tattoos, how did I miss noticing this part of the culture of my adopted nation in my last sixteen years here?

Then another truth about Seattle women dawned upon me. In addition to their intellect and creativity, they also have a good understanding of the laws of thermodynamics. In hot summer, they reduce the amount of fabric between their skin and the air, allowing the perspiration to evaporate efficiently, thus cooling the human body in a natural way. In the process, their tattoos become a tad more visible to the general population. Cool! I have chosen the right place to raise my daughters. In Seattle, they will grow up to be intelligent, creative, and scientific!

So what about Seattle men? Well, Seattle men are more into body piercing.

Once again, our NDA prohibits me from revealing the exact number of guys with piercings in my all-male engineering team at Amazon. I will say, though, that I am definitely proud to be leading a team of people who are not only highly intelligent but also very creative in their self-expression.

Shorts are very popular among men at Amazon during our hot and sunny summers. I have never been in a company where so many male executives — including the CIO, SVPs, and many of the VPs — wore shorts to work. Obviously, most of the engineers do so too. That does make Amazon a somewhat hairy place to work.

Another thing one notices about Seattle men is that a lot of them work in Amazon's engineering department—too many, one concludes, when one compares the demographic characteristics of Amazon's engineering department with that of the general population. Now, being a software type, I have worked under unusual demographic conditions for almost all of my professional life. But Amazon's engineering department demographics were much more skewed than that of not only Silicon Valley but also Delhi, Bangalore, Germany, Kentucky, and Tennessee. Under the usual circumstances, the 3:1 female majority at my home counter-balances the negative effects of such an environment. But at Amazon, I was living away from my family of females.

And I missed them - I missed my "girls", all three of them.

The Hacker Who Loved Me

Hacking is not a good thing, no sir! Whether you are a middle-aged gray-haired executive, a teenager, a mom juggling her career with taking care of her kids, or a retired police officer, you must absolutely resist the temptation to hack into computer systems. Hacking is nothing to feel proud of—not even if you are a teenager and believe yourself to be a very talented hacker. But views change if the talented hacker is a loved one and is able to break into the world's largest ecommerce company before you can drink your cup of coffee.

When I arrived at Amazon, they were all excited about rolling out a new web-based recruiting system. Their enthusiasm surprised me. Both of my previous employers of Amazon's size had implemented such a system way back in 1999. So what was the big deal? Given that Amazon was an Internet company; it only made sense that it implemented a web-based hiring workflow. However, this system was not a software package. It was actually built in-house by a developer-turned-manager who developed it on the side, in addition to doing his regular job. Now that was impressive.

One of my daughters was visiting the next weekend. I showed her around my new office. I also decided to take that time to enter into the new recruiting system my feedback for an interview I had conducted. She asked me what I was doing, so I proudly showed her the system. I brought up my own personal data record and pointed out how the system was implemented with controls so that I could only see my résumé and the names of the interviewers; but naturally, their feedback was hidden. The word "hidden" was marked as a hyperlink. She asked me to click on it, and I did. A popup came up, listing the three reasons for hiding the feedback from me. At that point, I went out for coffee and a cup of hot chocolate for my daughter.

When I came back, she was giggling. I prompted her for the reason and she pointed to the screen and said that the feedback from the interviewers who had interviewed me was very funny! What? Apparently, in the few minutes I was away getting coffee, she had broken into Amazon's recruiting system. When I asked her how she did it, she explained how she was able to fool the system into believing that she satisfied the three conditions, and how the system helped her break into itself by telling her the reasons why it was hiding the feedback. She also pointed out that the programmer had forgotten to code for the most important reason, reason number one. [Note: Details omitted on purpose – we don't want to embarrass Amazon, at least, not too much!]

I was horrified! I scolded her. She retorted that it wasn't as if she had broken into Amazon's PeopleSoft system and changed my salary. I was aghast. How did she know Amazon used PeopleSoft software for HR? And what does she know about PeopleSoft security anyway? And then I remembered how she knew. I used to work for PeopleSoft in Silicon Valley and one evening I saw her in my home office intently reading documents about PeopleSoft roles, permissions, and security.

Anyway, my interview feedback was all there in front of me, and I could not resist the temptation to read it. At twenty pages, it was bigger than any single story I had ever written. Those twenty-three author-interviewers, while writing their feedback about me, ended up writing a story that described them more than it described me.

One aspiring young immigrant was full of respect for another immigrant who had succeeding in rising through the glass ceiling. An older interviewer acknowledged his contemporary's wisdom and experience. Smart young Turks were exasperated with all the talking I had done about my experience. And finally, an impressionable young mind was surprised and amazed by the fact that, despite years of working in management jobs, my rusty old brain was still able to process technical details.

I must also admit that I could not resist the temptation of printing the feedback for reference whenever I needed a chuckle. After all, I was still a bit bruised from the grilling I had gone through during my interviews, including that one long session about secure HTTP protocol.

As I looked at the hacker who loved me, I simultaneously felt pride and embarrassment. Pride in my 13-year-old daughter who was able to break into a system built by the world's leading internet experts and embarrassment by the ease in which she practiced her skill right under my nose in my workplace while I fetched her hot chocolate.

Pick, Pack and Ship—Delivering Billions of Dollars to Investors

June 2003, Fernley, Nevada

I am at Amazon's largest fulfillment center, one of the 19 or so across the country. These are also called distribution centers or warehouses. Amazon requires all of its managers and supervisors to work in a warehouse as part of its C2 training. C2 stands for "customer connection." The program's origin lies in the early days of Amazon, when it could not afford to hire additional workforce to take care of peak demands during the holidays, so everyone in the company was required to pick, pack, and ship in the warehouse or to handle customer calls or e-mails. This practice stopped when Amazon grew, as it just became impractical. But then, a warehouse worker mentioned to Bezos that he missed the high-profile people coming down and working side by side with them during the crunch. Apparently, the mingling across the organizational boundaries inspired a feeling of camaraderie and it soon became clear that there were other advantages to the company when people in management roles had firsthand experience in core operations. Warehousing is at the very heart of the retail side of its business; and Amazon is all about picking, packing, and shipping goods. Hence, the C2 program today.

I liked the idea. We, the people who manage other people, should know how things operate at the worker level so that we can make better decisions. And of course, Amazon had created a lot of buzz about its fully automated warehouses, so I was curious to see one as well. Even though my software development group was working on the user and merchant interfaces, not inventory management or distribution software, I wanted to go through this experience.

The fulfillment center at Fernley, Nevada, is Amazon's largest. It spans thirteen football fields—so huge that part of it is in Utah. This was the ideal arena for Bezos to incorporate his algorithmic, metric-driven view of the company—a business that can be run by measuring and calculating everything. I arrived at 7:45

a.m., which, having been a computer programmer (or a supervisor of programmers), was a tad early for me. But the parking lot was packed.

Craig Conway, PeopleSoft's CEO, always used to say that you could tell who your best employees were by looking at the parking lot at 7 a.m. and 7 p.m. He said that the vast majority of people who come early are also the ones who go home late and those people were your best employees. If he had been the CEO of Amazon, he would have been very proud of his workforce! But I digress. Entering the building and glancing around, I saw a sign that said "Customer Connection Orientation, 2nd floor." Well, that was my cue. I found the elevator and walked in with a group of people. The door shut, and I noticed that the only button pushed was for the second floor. As the elevator began to rise, the conversations indicated that the people in the elevator were from all areas of the company. We entered a conference room and were handed a thick 200-page binder. I was a bit disappointed. I wanted to spend more time on the floor, not going through a series of PowerPoint slides.

A young guy moved in next to me. He was dressed in jeans and a tee shirt, and he had a backpack that he laid right at my feet. Once we were all settled, he introduced himself saying, "My name is Dave. I'm the leader of the customer connection team, and I would like to welcome this week's C2 program participants!" We were asked to introduce ourselves as well. "Tell us, what your name is. What is your title? Your responsibilities?"

The information binder revealed several interesting things. No, I am not going to divulge any proprietary information. I will mention things in generalities, such that, any information I am giving out here had been released to the public sometime over the past ten years in some form or the other, though you may have to search hard to find it. The first thing on the agenda was safety, followed by a tour of the gigantic warehouse and a description of the process flow; and finally, two-hours of training on the scanner.

In place of an hour-by-hour description of my training, I will just go ahead and describe the warehouse. The first thing you notice when you enter the warehouse is its gigantic size. It looks really big from the outside, and once you enter, you become overwhelmed with a feeling of the triumph of man and machine over nature and, if you are a newly recruited Amazon employee, a strong surge of almost religious fervor, one that makes you want to laugh and cry at the same time.

As we walked around the warehouse, it became clear that Amazon had completed its transformation from an online bookseller to being a general store with more than twenty-two top-level categories. Consumer electronics had surpassed books as Amazon's largest sales category. In addition, Amazon was no longer just an online retailer, but a marketplace where other retailers sold their wares. The folks at the warehouse put special tape on the unopened crates of inventory belonging to other large merchants using Amazon as their fulfillment provider. These merchants included

Target.com and Toys "R" Us. [2] We were taken to the receiving portion of the warehouse where there were items from hundreds of suppliers making life for receivers a bit challenging. The scene at the warehouse was busy, but it looked very organized and controlled.

The design of the warehouse was such that it would confound any first-time visitor, but there was a method behind the madness. When goods entered the warehouse, they were sorted into orange plastic crates known as totes. A conveyor belt carried the totes to a giant pick tower where the Amazon staff began the work of picking (moving the goods to their proper place on the shelf). Each item had a barcode that told the system, and the staff, what it was and where it should be physically located. Without the barcode, though, it would be nearly impossible to locate any item in the warehouse because its location was calculated with complex algorithms that optimized shipping. These

---

[2] Toys "R" Us has since severed their relationship with Amazon after a contentious lawsuit between the two companies that concluded in 2006.

algorithms took into account the time to pick and pack
a particular item, its ordering frequency, and even
what items were usually ordered with it. The distance
from the mouth of an aisle and the location of the aisle
were also part of this computation. It meant that
inventory was in the right spot to ensure that workers
have ease of access to the right merchandise at the
right time and that a customer's order is shipped in a
single box when possible. This shrewd efficiency
allowed Amazon to reduce shipping prices.

The process of packing multi-item orders was
rather complex as every item was placed in a different
part of the giant warehouse. However, Amazon's
sophisticated systems simplified the process by helping
the staff to find the shortest route in gathering all the
ordered items. Once gathered, the items were then
loaded onto trolleys and moved on to the pre-sort
stage.

In the pre-sort process, also done in the giant
picking tower, the ordered items were again loaded
into the orange totes, with every tote containing two

or three orders, before being sent to the next step: sorting. The totes sent for sorting were filled with a hodgepodge of items because sorting is dedicated to separating the items in the totes and ensuring that they land into the right customer's box. The process of sorting was quite amazing to view. The items that arrived from the picking tower were sorted out into small compartments, with each compartment representing a single order.

Each order was then packed and transferred to the postal sorting operation where it was weighed automatically. It was fascinating to watch the brown boxes glide by, just like children on the slide in a playground. These customer boxes were then shifted by chutes, which ultimately sorted them for distribution. Items marked for gift-wrapping were separated to be wrapped while the others were sent for labeling and shipping. Workers loaded the picked and packed customer orders into company-owned trucks and drove them to nearby shipping hubs. This held down costs and saved time.

With such a large volume of items, bringing down the costs associated with picking, packing, and shipping is a major vehicle to improving margins and profitability. A shipping carrier's performance is measured at every hub. If one hub makes too many mistakes, Amazon stops sending packages there until performance improves. At the warehouse, the manager leaves visual cues to operational performance. For example, there are locations where workers put damaged, duplicated, or inaccurately picked items in a pile. This alerted everyone to how well—or how poorly—the processes were working.

Amazon's metrics-driven culture and its obsession with continuous improvements in the way that items were picked, packed, and shipped enabled them to break through the last significant barrier to the dubiously slim advantage that brick-and-mortar stores had over ecommerce: the cost of shipping. Bezos, being a clever CEO, made shipping Amazon's problem, not the customer's, and pushed his management think tank to continuously figure out ways of reducing shipping costs so that he could offer both the free super-saving shipping for orders over $25 and Amazon Prime, which covered two-day shipping for everything a customer orders.

Amazon's relentless focus on automating and running its warehouse operations efficiently was a big step towards reaching profitability. In the early days, the warehouse operations were a substantial part of Amazon's cost—picking and packing cost as much as 15% of sales. Matters only became worse when Amazon expanded into toys and electronics because the early work in terms of moving items on conveyor belts and automatically packing them was focused on media products, books, CDs and DVDs.

However, by the time of my visit, Amazon's warehouses had become the most advanced distribution centers in the world; they hummed like an intelligent machine. The software not only routed an order to the handheld computing device of the worker nearest to the pick location, it could also take traffic into account by anticipating where bottlenecks were likely to occur and moving people around to avoid them. It also periodically calculated which products were most in demand and thus should be placed at the front of supply lines, increasing the speed of the flow.

The results were simply spectacular. Amazon's distribution centers in 2003 could handle triple the volume of six years before at half of the cost – only 7.5% of revenues while also reducing the number of picking and packing errors by half. This automation was part of the reason that Amazon had close to four billion dollars in revenues for fiscal year 2002 becoming profitable on a quarterly basis in Q4. This caused a big jump in its market valuation, delivering billions of dollars to the investors who had stood by Amazon during the dot-com bust that had started in 1999 and was just coming at an end.

Crossing Borders

Bezos had started Amazon as Earth's largest online bookstore. However, books were just incidental to his larger ecommerce vision; books were a needed first step. He spent four days taking the Prospective Booksellers School seminar sponsored by the American Booksellers Association. While the students learned to set up small, independent bookstores, none realized that Bezos was going to put them out of business.

While he was working at the global investment firm D.E. Shaw, Bezos compiled a list of products that could easily be sold on the internet. When he was ready to expand Amazon beyond the book market, he worked from that original list. Amazon started to sell DVDs as its second product; but music was also part of his vision. Bezos saw that the value of the existing infrastructure and customer base would multiply as we moved to sell more types of products.

Building Earth's biggest online store also meant building the brand. Bezos believed a good brand involved a promise and that the company needed to deliver on that promise to protect its brand. One of the essential dilemmas in building the Amazon brand image was how to present the "Earth's Biggest Online Store" as a good guy, rather than a Goliath that everyone would want to see fail. The internet marketing firm, USWeb/CKS[3], was brought in for online marketing strategy. The agency worked hard to give Amazon's brand a cool sense of humor. For example, they emphasized the breadth of Amazon's title list with ads like "XXX books on Marxists, including XXX on Groucho."

But Amazon did not just focus on monetizing its brand reputation and marketing prowess, it also offered a marketing fee to affiliates who brought customers to Amazon. While many ecommerce companies have affiliate programs, Amazon's is the most extensive whereby hundreds of tools and widgets

---

[3] USWeb/CKS and Whittman-Hart merged in March 2000 to form marchFIRST, Inc. In April 2001, marchFIRST went bankrupt.

are provided to their affiliates. This included simple image and text-based product links so that an author or musician, for example, could link a book or CD on his or her website, as well as banner ads, scrolling photo galleries, Ferris Wheel widgets, video widgets and more. There was even a customizable affiliate web store that could be branded, but was operated by Amazon behind the scenes. The affiliate program was innovative enough that it was granted a patent in the year 2000.

The members of this program are independent organizations that range from non-profit to for-profit companies whose primary business is not ecommerce. Amazon's affiliate program allows them to have a separate stream of revenue. The affiliates receive commissions ranging from 4 to 15 percent, depending on the product category and the performance of the third-party seller. The affiliate program has a staggering 900,000 members who sell products for Amazon.

By 2003, Amazon had already solidly established itself in the books, movies, and music markets. Around the time I joined Amazon, Tower Records and Sam Goody's, two strong players in the music retail industry were filing for bankruptcy and closing stores and while the advent of downloadable music was partially responsible, so was Amazon. And to add an additional dimension to the platform, Amazon had expanded to multiple countries by establishing subsidiaries in Canada, UK, Germany, France and Japan.

J.K. Rowling's *Harry Potter* series brought forward the issue of cross-country commerce where books published in one country and distributed in another had multi-million dollar implications. By 2003, 20% of Amazon's revenues came from overseas. Bezos spoke proudly of how Amazon was helping to educate the world by shipping books to places where there was no other way of getting books. However, some of these entries into the world market were beset by controversies. The one in Canada faced steep opposition from the Canadian bookseller's associations. Finally, a quid pro quo kind of policy arose between the

Canadian government and Amazon; the former approved Amazon's application only when Amazon promised that it would promote Canadian culture, provide increased exposure for authors in Canada, and make an investment of $20 million to assist local authors and publishers.

Amazon also had its eyes on the fastest growing economy in the world—China. In 2004, Amazon acquired the Chinese online bookstore Joyo.com for $75 million in stocks and in cash. Joyo.com was the largest online bookseller in China, and just like the Amazon, it had product lines that ranged from music to DVDs to other consumer goods.

Considering the intensity of the market in China, Amazon left no stone unturned and pumped most of its sophisticated technology into that site, which then became known as Joyo Amazon. In 2006, Joyo Amazon was rebranded and several new categories were added. It now operates under the name of Amazon.cn.

Research indicates that Amazon generates $750 million in online sales in China, and that is expected to reach $1 billion in the coming years. Considering this success, Amazon began to count the active users in China, which it says stands at a staggering 114 million.

All in all, Amazon's strategy to get involved in international market early has paid off. Amazon's growth in US retail operations had beginning to slow down in 2003 despite its continued expansion into additional product categories. Even though the market place operations in US were picking up pace, Amazon needed to make significant additional investment in R&D and operations. Growth in International retail operations, where in most cases, Amazon is the merchant, provided a welcome addition to Amazon's overall margin growth.

Amazon continues to add additional new product categories to its existing foreign websites, and in 2011, when this book is being published, Amazon offers marketplace functionality, where 3rd party merchants can sell products side by side Amazon's offering has been rolled out to all its international sites.

The Inner Workings of Bezos' Bazaar

Having established supremacy in the BMVD (Books, Music, Video, and DVD) categories, Amazon began the process of transforming itself from an online retailer to an ecommerce platform. After all, retail is a thin-margin business. For instance, Wal-Mart, the world's largest retailer, has operating margins of less than 6 percent, while companies like eBay, who simply provide a platform for others to sell their products, maintain operating margins of 24 percent or higher.

Several large retailers were already using Amazon's technology to sell their products. The list included bigwigs in the retailing industry, companies such as Target, Nordstrom, and Land's End. In some cases, such as for Target, Amazon operated and maintained a customized website that carried the Target brand, not Amazon's. Target's orders were shipped from Amazon's warehouses, but with a packing slip imprinted with Target's name and Bullseye trademark, so the customer's experience was as if the product came directly from Target. However, this model does not scale well. It would have been difficult to clone Amazon's website and offer customized packing and shipping for thousands of merchants. Besides, large retailers had already invested in sophisticated warehouses of their own. So for the next level of retailers, Amazon switched to the marketplace model.

Since Amazon had a highly scalable technology platform, as well as millions of customers, it was only natural to leverage those assets and not be limited by its origin as a retailer. Amazon had already gained an excellent reputation for world-renowned customer service, speedy shipping, and "Earth's largest selection"; and an association with Amazon would bring value to any merchant. A new path to greater profit would be forged by leveraging technology and brand reputation to build a marketplace that was better than any other marketplace on Earth.

While in 2003 Amazon was not yet profitable year-round, its nemesis, eBay, which had gone public years after Amazon, was already profitable. It had a market capitalization that was three times that of Amazon. With no inventory risk, and no capital expenses, depreciation or interest associated with building and operating giant warehouses, eBay seemed to have found the magic formula for success in an ecommerce company.

One of the initial competitive strategies Amazon carried out was to mimic eBay by creating Amazon Auctions, which failed miserably. Unfortunately, the millions of customers who went to Amazon to buy products were not interested in its auctions. Amazon then purchased LiveBid.com, a three-year-old Seattle-based company that broadcasted live auctions on the Web, for an amount that is undisclosed.

But by 2003, the strategy to mimic eBay was obviously not working and the best bet was to build up on Amazon's core strength: a powerful catalog system supported by a sophisticated item authority process whereby product data from various suppliers was combined in such a way as to populate the catalog with most trustworthy and complete information. When product information was combined from multiple sources, each attribute of the product was evaluated, one by one, and the most reliable one was selected.

Meanwhile eBay was copying some of Amazon's features, such as fixed price listings. Although people think of eBay as an auction site, its "Buy it now" option made it a marketplace in a standard retail model where there is a fixed price. In addition, eBay had acquired Half.com, which featured transaction fees on standard items, similar to the sales model of Amazon. And eBay had started to build a rudimentary catalog system similar to Amazon's for popular items, which simplified the process of listing a product for sellers. Both Amazon and eBay had launched a web services program for developers where applications could be built around their APIs.

The Amazon Marketplace was a major turning point towards improving margins. Amazon's marketplace is a site where any business, with some rare exceptions such as pornography, firearms, tobacco, and live animals, could list its products on Amazon's website. For obvious reasons, merchants were carefully screened in categories such as apparel, personal and healthcare, and gourmet food. If a merchant wasn't equipped to process sales transactions over the internet, Amazon would automatically fax the orders for an additional fee. Amazon was the middleman, providing the connection between the buyer and the seller. A marketplace is somewhat analogous to a mall, where you can buy products from various merchants. But the mall analogy breaks down quickly because products from different merchants were (virtually) placed next to each other so consumers could do easy, side-by-side comparison-shopping. Customers came to Amazon.com to look for items, find them, select them and pay for them using Amazon's online payment processing, with the order sent electronically to the seller.

To keep the customer service standards of third party sellers in the marketplace as high as Amazon's, sellers submitted to a strong system of customer reviews and several different metrics including order cancellations due to lack of inventory, on-time shipments, customer returns, and claims filed with

Amazon. In addition, the data from the third party seller transactions informed Amazon on which products were hot and thus giving Amazon unprecedented materials for deciding its own assortment strategy.

By 2003, the marketplace accounted for only one-sixth of the total revenues, but it already contributed towards one-third of the profits. These numbers were only going to grow, allowing Amazon to move from Wal-Mart-like margins of 5%–6% to eBay-like margins of 20%–25%. Although the marketplace was already a big source of revenue, it still needed a lot of improvements and features to be competitive with eBay in terms of being attractive to small businesses.

The move to a marketplace model helped Amazon to become a selling platform that was far superior to eBay. The uniform item description ensured that the customer was looking at different prices for the same product, unlike eBay, where the customer had to go through the description of every listing with similar sounding titles to make sure it was actually an apples-to-apples comparison. Amazon's neck-to-neck pricing and the elimination of merchant-specified shipping and handling made it a reverse bidding system where every seller was encouraged to offer the product at a price lower than the current lowest price, thus benefiting the consumer. The combination of commissions and subscriptions ensured that Amazon would make pretty good money regardless of whether the customer bought the product from Amazon or from a third party merchant. The business risk in unsold inventory was reduced, while the product selection on the website was increased.

Amazon Advantage gave merchants without their own shipping facilities use of its world-class fulfillment system. Amazon would stock, pick, pack and ship the goods on behalf of its marketplace merchants. In this case, Amazon managed the entire sales transaction from start to end, and in return received a decent commission on the sale of each item, and in some cases, charged a monthly subscription fee so money was made even if the seller did not sell anything.

With a large database of customer purchase transactions for everything they want from whomever they want gave Amazon an unparalleled insight into consumer trends that gave rise to the art of personalized product recommendations, which in turn increased sales across categories.

Bezos had always strived to create the most customer-centric company in the world, a place where someone could purchase everything they wanted over the internet from Amazon or one of its third party sellers.

Allowing other sellers to use Amazon's software to sell their products is the equivalent of SaaS (software as a service), an emerging model in the software industry. In Silicon Valley, companies like Salesforce.com were pioneering the practice of operating software on behalf of customers and charging them based on their usage of a shared system, instead of selling perpetual licenses to customers, as Oracle and PeopleSoft had done for more than a decade.

"What gets us up in the morning and keeps us here late at night is technology," said our fearless leader, Jeff Bezos. "From where we sit, advanced technology is everything."

Reprogramming the Giant Machine

The year 2003 ushered in a great leap in Amazon's business model: the transformation from a retailer to a true marketplace. The division I joined at Amazon was the Merchant Platform Division. Its goal was to build a flexible ecommerce platform where merchants could come and sell their products. It sounds a bit like eBay, but what we were trying to do was more sophisticated, and unlike eBay, Amazon's systems already targeted established retailers and larger merchants.

What remained was to build a platform in which a small merchant could easily enter product information into the system. Amazon's Item Merchandising application, which was what my group managed, was initially built for the requirements of a large retailer, such as Toys "R" Us or Target. In a large company, not only is there a separate merchandising department, but also there are separate people assigned to entering different pieces of information. For example, the people who entered product images into the system used a separate set of screens from those who entered the product description, and the whole catalog was built in a batch process that ran overnight. Products entered during the workday became visible on the site the next day. Data entry errors required an additional day as they were fixed and run through the nightly batch process again.

While such a system worked for a retailer such as Target.com, it made Amazon very unattractive to the small sellers who preferred eBay's single page data entry application where everything about a product, its unique identifier, description, images, condition and price, was entered all at once on one page. It was also posted to the website instantaneously, giving the small seller instant gratification.

The transformation from a retailer to an any-sized merchant platform wasn't easy. All of the systems— from the front end (the website) to item creation, to catalog management, to warehouse operations and to shipping and receiving—needed to be re-engineered.

It meant that we had to reprogram all of Amazon systems, starting with the systems where items and prices were entered into Amazon's enormous catalog. We also reprogrammed its website, where items were displayed in stores within the store, as well as the systems where payments needed to be tracked and sent to participating merchants. After an order was booked, the system had to distinguish between orders to be shipped by Amazon from the orders that would be shipped by participating merchants who needed the order sent by e-mail or file transfer systems.

I managed the item merchandising group at Amazon. My team developed various applications related to items, including item creation, classification, and display. Amazon has millions of items in its catalog, which belong to hundreds of thousands of categories and sub-categories. The origins and demographics of these items had been rapidly changing over the past few years, requiring many modifications to the system as the transformation to an ecommerce platform began.

In the beginning, the majority of the items sold at Amazon were native to Amazon. They were purchased by Amazon's buyers and were defined and created in the catalog by Amazon's merchandisers. With the doors open to third party sellers, Amazon would become a universal ecommerce platform, where every aspiring item could succeed based on its merchantability, independent of its origin.

Zillions of new items, which belonged to gazillions of categories, that didn't look like the Amazon's native items (books, music, videos, or DVDs), had to have an identity of their own. And they had to be handled differently. They could not always be treated like the majority, but they still added a lot of value and provided a vehicle for Amazon's growth. Assimilating these items into Amazon's website took some rethinking. Systems had to be redefined with added flexibility to classification methodologies in order to accommodate the differences among zillions of items.

Amazon was proud of the fact that it had "stolen" a top executive from Yahoo in Silicon Valley. Udi Manber, a famous search technologist of Israeli origin, was given the title of Chief Algorithm Officer. He was chartered to lead Amazon's entry into the search business, starting with the Search Inside the Book project. I soon realized that as a former Silicon Valley executive, I was also showcase material for Amazon. This was supposed to be a sign of respect, but it also came with lots of expectations and responsibilities.

I was given the ambitious assignment of unifying Amazon's internal item merchandising system and the browsing systems used by the consumer. At the same time, I had to make them both flexible enough to allow the launch of new online stores ranging from Jewelry to Sporting Goods to Gourmet Food. The addition of each new store brought in hundreds of new merchants and millions of new items that had to be classified into thousand of new categories and sub-categories.

The whole taxonomy—the classification system—needed to be very flexible and fluid. We had to consider not only what products or categories already existed in the catalog but also how it might change in the next day, week, or month. The browsing structure needed to become fluid enough to handle sudden and unexpected explosions in the number of items in categories and sub-categories by new merchants, who sometimes added tens of thousands of items into obscure sub-categories such as "T-shirts with humorous prints." Unlike books, for which classification systems have existed for centuries, items such as clothing, sporting goods, and gourmet food needed innovative thinking about the best way to organize them so that customers could easily find what they are looking for.

What is the best way to organize a browse tree for sports apparel in an online sporting goods store? Should it be organized first around sport-themed categories, such as baseball, soccer, and basketball with an apparel section in each of those sub-categories? Perhaps there should be sub-sub-categories for men's, women's, and children's apparel? Or should apparel appear as the high-level category with men's, women's and children's as sub-categories and with each sport types as the sub-sub-category? Or should it be all of the above?

Among all of the projects in the transformation, Project X was the most interesting. It was about introducing an innovative way of creating information for cross-linking items, which could have a huge impact on Amazon's infrastructure and website. There were several elements of semantic web and artificial intelligence in it.

During a presentation, Jeff, Amazon's famous CEO, asked my manager how Project X aligned with the Supreme Project. The Supreme Project was an initiative sponsored by Jeff himself and it appeared that Project X competed with it. Now obviously, you can't have a project competing with the CEO's pet project.

"I won't be able to fly home this weekend," I told Sonia, my lovely wife, over the phone. "I need to fix a vision-alignment problem with one of my projects."

Sonia fully understands how important it is to align with the CEO's vision. She moved in executive circles when I became one in Silicon Valley years ago, and she had seen many a promising executive's career go nowhere because his or her vision was not aligned with the CEO's.

It took me the entire weekend to align the visions. For a time, it seemed like there were too many snags, that it was not possible to align the two projects. Finally, I used an old trick—split the project into two parts. Call one the "infrastructure" and call the other the "application". Then position Project X as the infrastructure and underplay the details of the application, emphasizing that Project X, the infrastructure, can be used for any number of applications, including the Supreme Project. Voila! Project X was no longer competing with the Supreme project! In fact, it was now complementary to it.

With Project X saved, at least for the time being, I badly needed a smile. I had been without one for a couple of weeks.

Journey to the Queendom

Finally, time to fly back to home! When I came through the door, my younger daughter, Not-So-Shy, squealed with joy and started running around me in circles. Her older sister, Shy, brought a project for me to look at. The mother stood by the side, waiting for her turn.

Not-So-Shy did not like her sister getting all the attention, so she tried to push her sister away from me. When that did not work, she started kicking her. Ouches, screams, and eventually, tears followed that struggle. When I was young and a nerdy college student I had always dreamed of pretty girls fighting over me. That dream had finally come true.

That afternoon, a shriek came from the bathroom. Not-So-Shy had recently become potty-trained and it seemed something in the bathroom had troubled her. This was followed by the sound of little feet running. She gave me a dirty look, pointed a finger at me, and warned me by saying, "Don't you ever leave the toilet seat up."

An artistic depiction of my younger daughter,
"not-so-shy"

She was right; in a female-majority household, the toilet seat should always be down.

Later that night, after the girls went to sleep, my wife and I talked about Amazon. I explained how I was given a door to use as a desk. I shared a tiny office with an officemate. It was an office so small; he had to get up if I wanted to go to the restroom. I discussed the really cheap stationery, the cheap-looking coffee and coffee cups in the kitchen, and how everyone worked long and hard hours while believing they were part of a revolution.

She was surprised that a company with billions of dollars in revenues and the best technical resources in the world would treat its employees like this. I explained how Amazon, like its founder Bezos, seemed to be going through a midlife crisis. It was a large multibillion-dollar corporation, but continued to act like a young company, a startup.

Sonia slept in my arms with a smile on her face, like a happy baby. After I had put my eldest girl to bed, I wondered if Sonia still admired me. Winning admiration from thirty-something women living in Silicon Valley is an extremely difficult proposition. When they're in their 20s, earning admiration from a woman is simpler. All you need to do is be a hot dude or get a lucrative job as an engineer at a hot company.

Winning admiration from thirty-plus women is much more challenging, especially if they live in Silicon Valley. You still must be tall, dark, and handsome. But in addition, you must also be successful in your career. At the boom time, this meant either being a director or a vice president or making at least a million dollars with your stock options. Thirty-plus women in Silicon Valley will forgive even a protruding belly or a balding hairline if their mates are executive vice presidents or CEOs.

By getting a decent job in a high-profile company, I had so far avoided disappointing the most important thirty-plus Silicon Valley woman—my wife. Over the years, I had managed to win admiration from her. But of late, it had become difficult. Winning her admiration, at the high cost of living away from home and trying to fit in with the cultish young Turks at Amazon, hadn't been all that easy. Oh well, whatever it takes! I was born a man of tradition and programmed by genetics to take care of my family and earn a living. Still, I boarded the flight next evening to return to Seattle with a heavy heart.

Not-So-Shy in Seattle. Photo by Kalpanik S.

The Summer Euphoria

Seattle is sunnier than San Francisco in summer,

since the days are much longer because of the higher

latitude. How long? The sun rises at 4:30 a.m. and sets at 10 p.m. Because of the long summer days, there is still enough daylight to go for a walk on the waterfront after my workday ends at 7 p.m. Some of Seattle's most famous tourist spots, such as Pike Place Market and the Space Needle, are within walking distance from my apartment.

Amazon's annual summer picnic was much anticipated in the company because it was the one time when Jeff was accessible to everyone. He participated in a dunking game, where he stands above a giant water container and people throw sponge balls at him, which he tries to dodge. If someone hits him, he falls into the water. It sounded silly to me, but everyone thought it was great fun. In practical terms though, the picnic was one of a few opportunities for staff from different buildings to get to know each other.

The picnic takes place on a farm outside of Seattle, in North Bend, Washington. The city of North Bend, 30 miles from Seattle, boasts of scenic views of the Cascade Mountains and "the most famous and popular hike in Washington State." The Mount Si trail is eight miles round-trip with a 4,000-foot change in elevation. North Bend also has a factory outlet mall and a historic downtown. It clearly thrives on tourism and recreation.

The company picnic offered go-karts, free beer, hayrides, hiking and the dunking booth where Jeff Bezos and other executives are the dunces. Miniature golf is played with pool cues at pool table height. Food included gyros, chicken, and strawberry shortcakes. The family-friendly picnic has a huge toddler play area with a climbing wall and water rides. Children are given free kites.

One of the most memorable amusements is the broomball tournament. Amazon broomball should not be confused with official broomball as defined by the International Federation of Broomball Associations. That broomball is played on ice with everyone wearing pads. Broomball at Amazon is played more like field hockey with a beach ball. Different departments at Amazon formed teams for the tournament. Each team had nine players and each player wore war paint.

Drinking beer was expected. Broken bones were a known hazard of the game. Department managers would get the company art department to make professional posters to recruit players for their team.

The picnic is a summer event that is very appealing to newcomers trying to find their place, and it seemed to provide good dating opportunities for the singles in the Amazon staff. It was fun, but I wished my family were there to enjoy it with me and I wondered what the locals did for fun in the summer.

In my research for the true soul of Seattle, I discovered Capitol Hill. The Seattle Virtual Tour claimed, "No neighborhood in the city has a more diverse population than Capitol Hill. Seattle's twenty- and thirty-somethings of many races and grunge rockers share the area with long time residents ensconced in the historic mansions." The Seattle Times said, "This evening, the tattooed and pierced denizens of Capitol Hill will venture out into closed-off streets for the seventh annual Block Party." Tattooed and pierced denizens? Twenty- and thirty-somethings of many races? That sounds so much like my fellow Amazonians. I must go to this party!

My brother was visiting from out of town, and I convinced him to accompany me. The streets were closed off as promised, but the traffic lights were still blinking on and off, adding to the party's aura of mystique.

A Seattlite welcomes us the Block party. Photo by Kalpanik S

There were several makeshift stages erected right in the middle of the street. There was plenty of food and beer and some guns—water guns, that is.

Several women were dressed as if they were going to a "Girls Gone Wild" party.

And people were singing and dancing, making Seattle look like the happiest place on Earth. Later, during the nine-month-long "gray season", I came to understand that Seattle does not have a fall, winter or spring—just a three-month-long summer and those nine months that we don't talk about. On this night, though, Seattle was at the height of its summer euphoria.

I looked at Seattle's glittering skyline on one side and its beautiful waterfront on the other, and asked myself the same questions I had asked about San Francisco sixteen years ago: *Will Seattle accept me or will its people treat me as someone different, not one of them?*

Can I accept Seattle and call it my home?

Right then, she appeared from nowhere as if the city had sent her to answer my questions. She was in her mid-20s and had the freshness that comes with such a young age. Her simple white dress accentuated her innocence. She looked young but, surprisingly, still understood that the most attractive thing a woman can reveal is her smile. Her friends giggled as she approached me with a bashful smile, reached for my hand, and insisted in her musical voice, "Come, and dance with me. You must!"

Photo by Kalpanik S.

As many of you know firsthand, this is a challenge men of my age face almost every day, in all major cities. What makes attractive young women spontaneously ask us to dance with them on the streets? Is it because we seem distinguished with our slightly graying hair?

I usually turn them down politely. After all, distinguished gentlemen who are away from home have more important things to do than to dance with pretty girls on the city streets. But I hesitated this time, and argued with myself. *Maybe this is an important local custom, an ancient Seattle ritual. But what if the next step of the ritual requires sacrificing the subject to Mt. Rainier?*

She became impatient with my distinguished deep thinking, so she grabbed my hand and pulled me with the full force of a determined woman. She turned out to be a very energetic yet graceful dancer. Her rhythmic movements were a celebration of life itself. Watching her dance was like watching a butterfly flapping her wings or a flower growing in fast motion. Soon, the rhythm and the magic of the moment got to me. The tech bubble may have burst and I was no longer a hotshot thirty-something vice president, but at that moment, the only thing that mattered was the beat and the rhythm of the music.

She kept dancing, moving, twirling, and twisting. As the music slowed down, she put her arms behind my neck and drew me close—Sonia would have said too close—causing my arms to automatically circle around her tiny waist.

Dancing in Seattle, Photo by a Passerby Volunteering to Take a Photo

Her reassuring smile answered my questions: Yes, Seattle would accept me as a new resident. And yes, I will be treated differently, because I am different—but that is not necessarily a bad thing. Because of my unique look and accent, curious young women will sometimes insist on sharing a few moments of their journey with me. And wise men with gray hair will sometimes offer me jobs because I say and do things differently.

As the sun went down, the goddess of dance continued to create poetry with her movements. When the music accelerated, so did she, with the energy of the water at Snoqualmie Falls, rushing with the vigor of youth.

The Block Party continues with its entire rigor into the evening, photo by Kalpanik S.

Soon, I couldn't match her energy and began to slow down. She came close—Sonia would have said too close—and whispered in her sweet voice, "Thanks for dancing with me. I don't understand why all these people just kept watching us and didn't dance with us." People? Oh my God! Were there people around us? They must have been staring at us!

I looked around. A few people were looking at us, but they all had a matter-of-fact look on their faces, as if in Seattle, people of different races danced together on the streets every day. I fell in love with them. I fell in love with their tattoos and piercings—I was going to get some too! That was the moment when I accepted this city. I was ready to call it home.

Also that moment finally ended a 33-year argument with my brother. Since the day he was born, I have claimed that I was the better-looking one. That day, on the streets of Seattle, we finally had the proof.

Later that night, my true love, my beautiful California realtor, called to tell me that she had sold our California house, all by herself. What timing! I love this woman. As most of you know, I married my realtor to save on commissions.

Leaving One Land for Another

Leaving one land for another, Photo by Colin Zheng

From: Me
Sent: Monday, July 28, 2003, 9:26 PM
To: Silicon Valley
CC: My friends
Subject: Bye-bye

Silly Valley,

The time has come to bid you good-bye.

I will always fondly remember our early years

together; how I had fallen in love with you from 8,000

miles away, without even seeing you; and how I dreamt about you. I remember my excitement when I finally got to you.

But the last few years haven't been as much fun, Silly. We became affluent and mature, but somehow, somewhere, we lost the enthusiasm, the energy of youth, and our innocence and naïveté.

I hate to tell you this, Silly, but I have been seeing other places.

I have fallen in love with one of them. This place – Seattle - is full of enthusiasm, fun, excitement, energy, and even has a touch of innocent foolishness.

I am breaking up with you, Silly, and moving in with Seattle. I am really sorry, but I am only 37 and not ready for feeling old. Not yet.

At the end of the day, though, this is a business decision. You taught me well, Silly, and made me a businessman. You are a rapidly declining job market, Silly, and I am exiting you to leverage my brand in another market with greater growth potential. Good luck with everything.

Me

P.S. I am going to steal some of your best and brightest to join me in my adventures in yet another land. Don't take it personally; this is just business.

P.P.S. I will miss you.

Seattle Bridge, Photo by Colin Zheng

Lake Washington, Photo by Colin Zheng

The Oath of Allegiance

My heart was full of strong emotions. The day had arrived to take on the identity of my new homeland and to sever my final ties with the land where I grew up. My family had joined me, and we were ready to assimilate with the natives of our new land. I was both excited and saddened at the same time.

I waited in a queue with people belonging to all major ethnicities: Asian Indians, Chinese, Koreans, Filipinos, and Hispanics—and oh, I almost forgot, a few Caucasians as well. Most of us worked in the technology industry and all of us came here for a better future. We eagerly awaited the formalization of our assimilation into our new homeland. And finally, the very emotional moment arrived.

With several other Californians who had recently arrived in Seattle to join Microsoft, Amazon, or a few other companies, I swore:

I hereby declare, on oath, that I absolutely and entirely renounce all allegiance to California; that I will henceforth bear true faith and allegiance to the laws, constitution and businesses of the state of Washington; that I will support, honor, and be loyal to Washington, its businesses and its women; that I will drive carefully under wet and slippery conditions; that each time I make fun of the Northwest's rains, I will also mention its lush greenery, its spectacular snowcapped mountains and its pretty maidens; that I will change my browser's home page to MSN.com; that I will avoid flying with airlines that do not purchase their planes from Boeing; that I will drink at least 3 cups of Starbucks coffee a day; and that I take this obligation freely without any reservation, or purpose of evasion; so help me, God.

Can you believe it? Twenty-four of the 25 questions in the written test for my Washington driver's license were about driving in wet and slippery conditions. What part of the road is more slippery after it rains?

Which way do you steer when you skid on a wet road?
How much distance should you keep when it is raining?

The petite young clerk had long hair as dark as
Washington's cloudy skies during the winter and eyes
that sparkled like Lake Sammamish in the summer.
When she punched a hole through my California
driver's license, a sob escaped me; I could not hold
back the tears any longer.

She handed me a tissue (they stock boxes of them for
all newcomers to Washington state) and comforted me
in her soothing voice, saying "Don't worry, just give it a
few years, you'll get used to the rain. Everyone does."
Her voice had the reassurance of the Northwest's
gentle streams, making my sadness vanish right away.

Seattle's Pretty Women, Photo Courtesy of Seattle's women commission

Changing Identity

From: Me
Sent: October 30, 2003
To: California
CC: My friends
Subject: Identity

Dear California,

I wanted to keep my California identity until it expired in 2005. No, that was not procrastination; it was sentimentalism. But the Seattle cops kept stopping me on the highways, claiming I was moving too fast. Playing the ignorant foreigner and pointing to the "90" in the I-90 sign did not work, and I was given ten days to give up your identity and get a Washington driver's license. Ten days! That's too short! But then, is even a lifetime enough to give up one's identity?

I must say, though, that I like my new digs with the view of snowcapped mountains and the beautiful Lake Sammamish, the lush greenery, the short commute, the fully paid-up house on the hill, and not having to pay any state income taxes. So the license with your name has gone into the box with four others. I am sorry, but I promise I won't just forget you like the other four places I have left behind. After all, what we had was special. You transformed me from a smart, shy young man to a wise, but still very shy, grown man. I promise I will sneak away from Washington every now and then to visit you and spend a night or two reliving the passions of our youth, the golden age of Silicon Valley.

Take care,

Me

Crossing the Median

It began like a normal business trip. I hugged my little girls, kissed my wife, and drove to the airport early in the morning. The sky was gray, and it was drizzling as usual. I flew back three days later, on a Friday evening and then, strange things started to happen, one after another.

To begin with, the gray clouds were gone, and there was a bright sun outside. A bright sun in Seattle? I panicked. I must have boarded the wrong flight! But then vague memories from last summer of a bright and sunny Seattle stirred in my mind. Maybe those memories were real, and those long sunny days were coming back? After all, the spring had officially started before I left.

Then, I couldn't find my car in the parking lot. After all, it has had three different license plates in less than two years and now I couldn't remember the current one. When I did finally find it, I had to struggle with the lock. It seemed to have jammed. Eventually it gave in, though I had to use brute force. As I entered it, the car looked a bit different. After 20 minutes of driving, I realized that I had missed my exit and had to turn back.

Finally, when I arrived home the garage door wouldn't open with the remote. Strange! I parked my car in the driveway and walked toward the door. Surprisingly, the door was ajar and I made a mental note to give a lecture to my wife as I walked in.

The house looked different. There was a new sofa set in the living room and a new dining table in the dining room. Hmm, my wife had been talking about getting some new furniture for a while, but how did she get it this fast?

Two pretty, young college students were over a laptop in the kitchen. Though they had their backs to me, it was easy to infer their ages from their fashionable, youthful clothing, and their slender, athletic builds. They were in their late teens or early twenties—yes, college students, or maybe young professionals. Both girls had beautiful, long, dark hair and wore trendy tops with low-rise cargo pants that revealed bare feet, a little leg, and hint of waist.

I realized with embarrassment that I had entered the wrong house for the second time in eight years! While my household also has a plurality of women, none of them was college aged. It also explained the problems with the garage door, the missed exit, and the new furniture.

Eight years ago, when my family and I were living in Redwood City, I arrived home one day to find that my sweet, beautiful, but always conservatively dressed, thirty-something wife was replaced by a bold, twenty-something, ultra-fashionable Latina. After a few seconds of watching the shocked expression on her face, I realized that I had entered our old apartment by mistake. We had vacated it a few days before and had moved to another apartment in the same building. By coincidence, our new apartment, #501, was right next to the elevators, just like our previous apartment, #201, three floors below. I had entered my old apartment by habit and I was looking at one of its new residents.

Yes, I must have entered the wrong house once again, so I quietly tiptoed out. Fortunately, both college students were so busy trying to figure out the wireless modem connection for their laptop that they did not notice my coming and going.

My heart beat rapidly, and my mind raced. Was I even in the right city? The names of the four cities I had lived in during the last eighteen months flashed by; Fremont, California; Nashville, Tennessee; Seattle and Bellevue, Washington. If my memory served me correctly, my current city of residence is in Bellevue. Was I in Bellevue? Or had I, in my absent-mindedness, boarded the wrong flight and returned "home" to one of those other three cities? The houses around me did not have stones or brick exteriors, so this wasn't Nashville. I looked across the road where a woman in the neighborhood was rushing towards her minivan. She was not Asian, so this was not Fremont, California. And this was definitely not Seattle! On Friday evenings in summer, young women in Seattle dress as if they were going to a party, whereas the woman across the road was dressed as if she were going to a PTA meeting. The "dressed for the PTA meeting" look confirmed that I was in suburban Bellevue.

So if I was in the right city, did I enter by mistake a house that looked similar to mine? You know how they build houses these days—they all look alike. I took out my spiffy new Washington state driver's license and checked the house number listed there. The number matched the one on the house I was standing in front of, and the street name matched the street sign.

My head started swimming. So this was the right house! But this whole thing was crazy. Where did these college students come from? What happened to the garage door opener? Why was there new furniture in our house? And, most importantly, where did my two little girls and my thirty-something sweet wife go? Then I realized with a shock that I must be in one of those crazy Sci-Fi scenarios and have traveled through a time warp into the future.

Well, I decided to make the best of the situation. Being in a time warp can actually be quite interesting. I decided to go in to say "Hello" to them. Even if I were caught in a time warp and accidentally traveled forward in time I would still be making acquaintances with two charming women of the future who were living in the same house in which I used to live in the past. Maybe they'll even sign up for my newsletter!

As I entered the door, I heard one female telling the other, "I told you so. Dad is back. I saw him going out." Dad? I looked at her. Yes, I was facing my daughter, 5-foot- 5-inches tall and a beautiful young woman with large pretty eyes and beautiful long hair. I was shocked. Call me conservative, but I really don't think a 13-year-old should have that kind of height— especially not while her father is out of town. And she was definitely too young to have those large pretty eyes and the beautiful long dark hair.

But kids these days don't listen to their parents anymore. While I was out, she decided to wait no more and grew into a young woman, with pretty, large eyes, long hair, and all the other physical manifestations of beauty. And where did the other young woman come from?

The second young woman was my wife. Women in Seattle start looking ten years younger in spring, as they shed their gray winter cocoons and start dressing for the hot summer. She had also lost some weight. Still, seeing mother and daughter together with identical height, style, and looks was a big shock—kind of like what Rip Van Winkle must have felt.

My wife claimed that this did not happen in the three days I was gone, but that it had been developing over the past few months. She pointed out that I'd been so busy in the last few months that I did not notice that our daughter was growing up, nor I had noticed that she herself had been slimming down. Finally, my wife informed me that even though we already spend more on our daughter's clothes and accessories than on hers, she still wanted to buy more and now had more makeup things than she had. She even wanted to buy a pair of fashionable boots; and when she was refused, she threatened to go directly to me and to buy it for her. She warned me that if I spoiled her by getting her that pair of expensive boots, I would need to get her a pair as well. If you got confused trying to tracking which "she" and "her" referred to whom, consider me—I have to disambiguate between her, her and her!

That night, I was very restless, but I kept on dreaming. In my dreams, I was putting up a tall iron fence with pointed spikes at the top around our house. It also had live electricity running through it. Will that be enough to keep the boys away? Also, in a second, parallel series of recurrent dreams, I was installing shoe rack after shoe rack while my youngest was crying nearby, demanding a pair of very expensive boots like her mother's and her sister's.

On my 38th birthday, I decided to go to Belltown, a hip Seattle neighborhood, to help me recover from the shock. I had stayed in a corporate apartment there last year and had fond memories of my stay, especially the spectacular show of body art put on by Seattle's pretty, young women. As I walked through Belltown, there came another big shock—the second one in two consecutive days. I suddenly realized that all the pretty, young women from last year were gone, and the streets were filled instead with delicate-looking daughters.

There were so many of them. They all walked like my daughter, giggled like her, and talked like her. And many of these daughters were as tall as my daughter, too. (Did I mention she is already a whopping five feet and five inches?) Some had the same large, pretty eyes as my daughter (though sometimes of a different color). Others had the same long hair, and many had the same shy-yet-playful smile. Most of these daughters were wearing fashionable clothes, and some had put on a spectacular display of artistic tattoos.

I realized that when a 12-year-old little girl suddenly shoots up to a height of five feet and five inches, the body and mind of her 38-year-old dad begins to go through a series of complex physical, chemical, and emotional changes. Gray hairs suddenly start showing up. The dark circles under the eyes become more prominent. The cheeks puff up a bit and all that weight he lost just last year starts coming back. He becomes very protective of the young and innocent. He joins the crowd of fathers protesting outside the teenager clothing stores. And he starts feeling fatherly feelings when he sees complete strangers.

This is a very strange feeling. Up until age eight, whenever I looked at a pretty woman, I wanted her to be my mother. For the next thirty years, I wanted her to be my friend, to go for tea, coffee, or beer together, and to tell her amusing stories about my adventurous journeys around the world. Now, all of a sudden, things have changed. I have some strange, new feelings for pretty women. I can no longer look at them without thinking about my daughter and the more delicate or innocent they look, the more I feel like bringing them a glass of milk and warm cookies instead of buying them a drink.

One unseen benefit to this whole they-remind-me-of-my-daughter thing is that I now have some conversation starters for attractive young women, such as "Your eyes are large and pretty, same as my daughter's" and "My daughter has beautiful long dark hair, which looks exactly like yours."

That sunny day in Bellevue, I crossed the median. I officially became older than 50 percent of the population in Bellevue, Washington[4].

---

[4] The median age of population of Bellevue, Washington is 38 years according to the US Census of 2000.

Leader of the Revolution

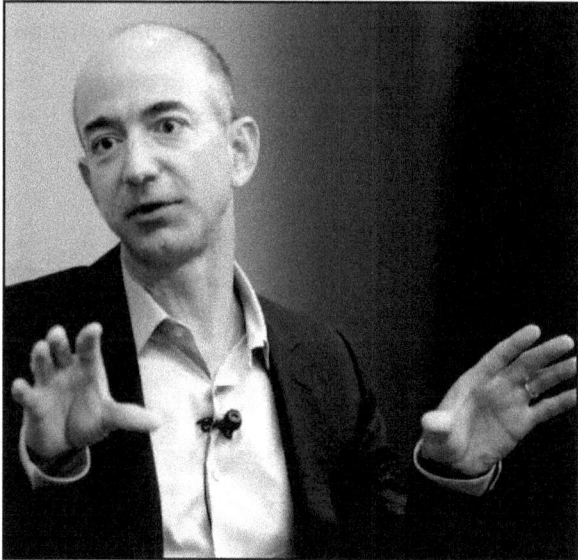

Bezos at Book Expo 2008. Photo provided by BEA organizers.

Jeff Bezos was a big part of my reasons for joining the Amazon team. Even though he was the CEO of a public company, he had no hesitation in acting like a 10-year-old kid. He had preserved that part of himself despite the trials that he and his company had gone through recently and despite the meltdown of the dot-com world—or maybe even because of it. His defiance appealed to me. He was my age, and I wanted to defy my age too. Like him, I wanted to defy the times—the downturn in the technology industry. I wanted to relive the passion of my youth, the golden nineties, when Silicon Valley was booming and the work was demanding, but the rewards were sweet.

Bezos and his first employees worked out of the garage of his home. He made his desk out of a door with 4x4 wood posts as legs. This desk became a symbol of the company's frugality. Bezos mentioned the desk in almost every interview and had it featured in a photo in Vanity Fair. Bezos was establishing a public image as a cool West Coast nerd, rather than an Ivy-League, Wall-Streeter and the desk helped to create his new image. Bezos' desk eventually found use as a promotional tool for the launch of Amazon's auction site. (His mother bought it.) Bezos' famous frugality continued even after Amazon's office moved out of the garage. He refused to spend money on fancy offices and furniture, insisting that the customer would never see them, and his golden retriever and other employee's dogs were given the run of the office.

Jeff Bezos came up with the concept of Amazon as an ivy-league graduate and Wall Street veteran and he hired people in his own image. The first two employees hired at Amazon were Shel Kaphan and Paul Barton-Davis. Neither man had experience with retail systems or business software programming. However, both men were brilliant and eager for new challenges. Kaphan had been involved in previous start-ups and flops, but Barton-Davis was leaving the comfortable University of Washington campus. Bezos had no interest in hiring anyone but the best.

Amazon applicants were expected to show creativity and innovation in everything they did. The approach to interviewing at Amazon was not centered on talking about previous experience, but on talking about hobbies, values, and hypothetical problems. The interview process was exhausting. Managers had to add interviewing on top of the 60 to 80 hour week of normal responsibilities, and each interview had to be documented and then followed up with half-hour conversations with all of the candidate's references.

Hiring decisions were made based on hundreds of pages of information about each potential candidate. To be hired, a candidate had to stand out in that haystack of information. Amazon asked applicants for their SAT scores and college grade point averages, as the company tended to hire Ivy League graduates and to look for other prestigious factors in the person's background. Amazon sent its recruiters to all the most prestigious universities looking for the "smartest."

In its carefully crafted legend, Amazon was born in a garage and launched with a word-of-mouth marketing campaign. However, the back-story reveals that the father of Amazon was a Wall Street insider who knew how to get investment from major players.

Bezos has described Amazon as "obsessively, compulsively, anal-retentively focused on customer service," but those adjectives could be applied broadly to the company's personality as well. As a retail company, Amazon needed the right kind of public image. Word-of-mouth publicity and customer loyalty depended on people feeling good about the company.

As Robert Spector says in his book *Amazon.com: Get Big Fast*, Bezos "has created an alternate persona (a variation on fact) that serves him well." The public Bezos is a prankster, a whiz-kid programmer with a warm smile and a unique sense of humor, while Bezos the CEO is a Wall-Street numbers guy who saw the potential of the Internet. Bezos often told people that Amazon wasn't making any financial projections. This may explain why the company attracted less venture capital than other 1990's dot-coms in the beginning.

Bezos became a great spokesperson for the company partly because he conveyed tremendous sincerity while only displaying the part of his personality that fit the company's public image. People noted Bezos' hearty, infectious laugh that clearly boosted company morale making Amazon a place where not only it was OK for employees to have fun, but where the CEO was visible symbol company's employee slogan – "Work hard. Have fun. Make history."

Close Encounter of the First Kind

After several years of trial and error, Bezos had finally realized that the real way to make money on the Internet wasn't by building large warehouses or using automated machinery to sort and ship books and DVDs. The emerging model was to leverage Amazon's scalable technology and allow other merchants to sell their wares and charge them a fee. So Amazon was now focused on promoting its sellers platform, and I worked for the newly formed seller's platform division.

I had been at Amazon for a few months when I attended the first-ever sellers' conference where the vice president of my division gave a presentation on the planned new features of the website, which would enhance the seller's experience. While the VP was engrossed in his presentation, Bezos entered the stage behind him, riding his Segway.

Bezos on a Segway. Reprinted under the fair use doctrine permitted by Section 107 of the U.S. Copyright Act.

As the VP turned every which way to find the source of the distraction in his presentation, Bezos dexterously maneuvered his Segway so that he remained hidden from the speaker, playfully annoying him. Then he burst out with a loud, booming laugh, like a small explosion. It was an unconstrained, non-stop laugh and it went on for quite some time. I could see why people compared it to a hyena's laugh, though I must admit I have never met a hyena, let alone heard one laugh. After thoroughly enjoying his childish prank, Bezos got down from his scooter and took a seat right next to me.

I was surprised at how ordinary he looked. He was a jovial, small, bald guy. The famous pioneer of e-commerce and founder of one of the pillars of the Internet wore baggy khakis and worn-out shoes. He looked thin, frail, and rather ordinary—one of the masses. He had an anti-charismatic charisma; a likable, normal person who had come up with a great idea and succeeded. He looked totally different from the other billionaire CEOs that I had seen up close, such as Larry Ellison at Oracle and Craig Conway at PeopleSoft. Larry and Craig were always meticulously dressed in Italian suits and expensive shoes, making them look larger than life.

The Cold, Calculating Machine

Behind the laughter and the easygoing personality, Bezos was an exceedingly demanding CEO who believed in a culture of metrics over everything else. His obsession with numbers had apparently managed to subdue his humane side making him a CEO devoid of any feelings of empathy.

I attended the annual company meeting where Bezos answered questions from employees. One question asked him to justify the annual "cruelty curve"

206 | The Cold, Calculating Machine

used in Amazon's performance review process. The cruelty curve is a system that forces managers to rank their employees in relative order of merit where the bottom 10 percent were put on a performance plan— and usually fired not much longer after that. Bezos defended this "rank and yank" system at Amazon by citing evidence that the system ensured that the talent at Amazon always remained top notch.

I could not believe it. Amazon was treating employees as mere statistics, and culling the weakest of the herd to improve the gene pool. I knew that companies such as GE followed such practices, but they were industrial conglomerates with a normal pool of talent—very different from the extraordinary mercenaries who were sacrificing their personal lives because they believed they were carrying out a revolution and changing the world. Because they believed in the cause, Amazonians sacrificed their personal lives to work extremely long, grueling hours in mousetrap-sized dark offices that made the garment factories in India seem palatial. Trust me; I know what a garment factory in India looks like because my brother owns one.

This was not how we did it in Silicon Valley! There, as a manager, I treated my team members as my colleagues, not merely replaceable components or statistics. Companies such as HP, Apple, and PeopleSoft have led the nation with their employee-friendly practices, believing that breeding loyalty and trust among the employees is the best way to increase productivity. Bezos intended to raise the quality of his staff by increasing its competitiveness from year to year.. "Culling the herd" (eliminating the lowest performing employees each year) added to the competitive atmosphere at Amazon.

My disillusionment in Bezos' leadership grew during an executive presentation from my division. One of my colleagues, John[5], was the director of the item management group. John and his team were responsible for managing the Amazon virtual catalog.

---

[5] "John" is a pseudonym.

He was very proud of his achievements over the previous few years at Amazon. As Amazon expanded from selling only books, to CDs and DVDs, then to selling electronics, apparel, sporting goods, jewelry, food, prescription drugs, home and garden products, and 40 other categories, it opened shop in five countries—USA, Canada, UK, Germany, and Japan—and turned from a retailer to a platform supporting thousands of merchants. John's group managed all of the product information for a vast range of items across all of the stores, markets, and sellers.

But that day, Bezos was livid. A seller had complained that the system did not handle a particular case of variations accurately—that is, items that are almost exactly like each other, differing only in some attribute such as color. During John's presentation, Bezos began to chew him out for missing that case in his system design. He kept emphasizing how 99.9999 percent accuracy wasn't good enough for a system with ten million items, since that will lead to ten errors.

After the meeting, John was in agony and I woke up to the realization that Bezos was obsessed with perfection and success. That in his quest for world domination, he had given up his humanity. I could see now that Amazon wasn't the next wave of technological revolution, at least not in the sense of how we did it in Silicon Valley in the last decade by providing a nurturing environment for employees. Instead, it was a giant, cold and calculating number-crunching machine.

A1, A2...A9

When I arrived at Amazon, there was a lot of buzz about Amazon's celebrity hire, Udi Manber, the big shot search scientist of Israeli origin who used to work for Yahoo. Udi was hired to be Amazon's Chief Algorithms Officer and had a special privilege in that he did not have to relocate to Seattle. I was envious of course.

Soon thereafter, Amazon launched a search subsidiary dubbed A9 and named Udi its CEO. In typical Amazon fashion, A9 was a cryptic abbreviation common among computer programmers that stood for A followed by nine characters ("Amazon" plus_ "." plus "com"). However, it's one thing to use a cryptic short name for an internal training program and completely another to use it to attract customers to a new service offering.

A9 was based in Silicon Valley where Amazon was fully intent on recruiting the talent from Google and

Yahoo. Its main accomplishment was to implement the "Search Inside the Book" feature.

One of the limitations in buying books on the internet is that people are not able to flip through the book and sample it the way that they can in a bricks-and-mortar bookstore. With Search Inside the Book, Amazon gave its customers the ability to flip through the first few pages of a book, as well as the capability to search within the book.

Searching inside a book is a very complex process that required digitalizing the content of the entire book. Unlike the internet, where web pages are stored and transmitted as digital encoded data, there is usually no digital master available for books. Most books are produced using a manual typesetting process, and even for the books that are digitally printed, the master is not easily available. Digitalizing a book involved scanning the book one page at a time, and then using Optical Character Recognition (OCR) to convert the scanned image of the page into a string of characters. OCR is an electronic process that decodes each character and then encodes to produce the text in a structured document form that makes it capable of being searched.

Udi and his team used the processing power of Amazon's mighty servers at off-peak periods, such as late at night when there were few people browsing Amazon's website and few orders going through the system. This helped Amazon save plenty of money, cutting back on the cost of buying separate hardware for the project.

But after the successful launch of Search Inside the Book, A9's vision began to peter out and Udi Manber, Amazon's celebrity hire, left Amazon in 2004 to work for Google.

Things Start to Fall Apart in Fall

I had a partner in the revolution. Julie[6] was the product manager of Project X and we jointly presented the status of Project X to the senior executives every other week. And every other week we both were mercilessly thrashed. Trust me, regular thrashings endured together builds a strong feeling of partnership between two people.

Julie was a product manager with an MBA from a famous business school. Even though she was twelve years younger than I was, a kinship and mutual feeling of respect had been built between us. She was an athlete and was training for a marathon, but despite her strength on the field, she was very gentle in person, unlike the assertive alpha males of Amazon. At Amazon, males outnumber females 10 to 1 in the

---

[6] "Julie" is a pseudonym.

software development department, and most of the few females that survived had adopted the alpha male assertiveness. Julie, on the other hand, believed in avoiding confrontation and spent endless time trying to build consensus. Amazon's alpha male-dominated culture in which confrontation was encouraged, viewed both actions as weaknesses.

Most meetings at Amazon resembled the daunting, stress-inducing oral thesis exams at major universities. Managers would present new ideas and strategies to implement their projects and then senior executives would ask questions with the skill of first-class prosecutors until they were satisfied that they had explored every angle. Unfortunately, in this style of management, it did not matter much whether the answer was correct or not. What mattered was how confidently you answered the questions.

Preparing for these long, oral exam meetings for multiple projects required long hours at work in an environment similar to a Third World factory. We were given an unfinished door as our desk and spent twelve-hour days in small dark offices. It was a complete contrast to the shining, large, and well-lit offices with glass walls in Silicon Valley. It made me feel as if I were trapped in a dark and gloomy matrix, a small dot in the giant structure of a large corporation. Despite the employee slogan to "Work Hard, Have Fun, Make History," I wasn't sure I was having fun at Amazon. We were driven hard and brutally, leaving hardly any room for fun.

Julie was visibly suffering. She believed that she was truly part of a revolution, and not just another venture to sell products to consumers. She pretended that she was having fun—but she really wasn't. No one was, at least in my department.

When fall arrived again in Seattle, Julie left Amazon. I walked with her to the elevators. She walked gracefully, with tranquility on her face and the gentleness of a child. I wished her good luck and raised my hand in a high-five-like gesture, my cultural adaptation for wishing someone good luck. She was surprised and amused by the unexpected gesture. She blushed, then smiled, and finally reciprocated by slapping my upraised palm. The elevator doors opened, and my first friend in Seattle walked away from me.

The sun hid behind the gray clouds as it prepared to go home. The skies, which had been clear, blue, and cheerful in summer, now appeared sad. Tears rolled down Seattle's cloudy cheeks, falling on its streets as drizzle. As the sun vanished behind Elliot Bay, the sky above Seattle turned dark and it rained throughout that black cloudy night. That dark rainy night marked the beginning of the end of the chapter on Amazon in the story of my life.

WINTER FREEZE

In the middle of the 2004 holiday season, visitors to Amazon.com were greeted with messages such as "Service unavailable" or "We are sorry." This was not the first time that Amazon had an outage, nor would it be the last. An Amazon insider blamed the complexity of the systems for the outage; the real picture was somewhat different.

This outage hit Amazon particularly hard. The holiday season was in full swing, and outraged sellers watched helplessly as their expected earnings faded away with the ticking of the holiday clock. The outrage increased when sellers realized that they were also unable to transfer much-needed funds from Amazon into their own bank accounts. Yet, despite the bashing and bad publicity, Amazon chose to keep mum about the real reasons that led to the outages.

In June and July of 2009, Amazon was plagued with more outages, this time with its cloud computing services, affecting many startups that relied on Amazon's storage services to store their data. Amazon was again reluctant to admit the problem that led to the outages, choosing instead to focus on a public relations campaign that glowed with optimism but provided no useful information. The statement from the PR team read:

> We've been operating this service for two years and we're proud of our uptime track record. Any amount of downtime is unacceptable and we won't be satisfied until it's perfect. We've been communicating with our customers all morning via our support forums and will be providing additional information as soon as we have it.

However, as usual, the real picture was something different. Amazon was so engrossed in expanding its business that all of its developers were working on new projects and without the proper resources to maintain and support the website, outages were a natural consequence. When support and maintenance was a priority, Amazon.com had a sterling reputation for reliability.

And then, the legal battles begin.

In 2000, Amazon and the retail giant Toys "R" Us joined forces. Together, Amazon and Toys "R" Us aimed to help parents like me find toys that would provide our kids with a learning experience that would match their interests and personal traits. Amazon managed the entire online shopping experience, which included website development, customer service, and order fulfillment, while Toys "R" Us did the buying, assortment planning, and inventory management for its toys, games, and children's furniture. At the time, it seemed like a match made in heaven.

However, the happy relationship between Toys "R" Us and Amazon lasted just three years. Toys "R" Us had agreed to pay Amazon a whopping $51 million per year to be the sole authorized seller of toys, games and baby products on Amazon.com. But in 2004, Toys "R" Us filed a lawsuit to cancel the stipulated ten-year, co-branded marketing deal stating that Amazon was not upholding its end of the agreement by allowing third party sellers of toys, such as Target, on the website.

Amazon, angered, filed a counterclaim alleging that Toys "R" Us failed to maintain the necessary inventory levels to meet consumer demand.

In 2006, the Court sided with Toys "R" Us and rejected Amazon's counterclaim. The Court terminated the partnership, but did not award damages to Toys "R" Us, so the battle was won, but the war was not over. Toys "R" Us continued the fight to recoup the losses it believed were incurred in its partnership with Amazon. Finally, in June 2009, Amazon agreed to pay Toys "R" Us $51 million to settle the lawsuit. The divorce was now final.

The Slacker Sun

From: Me
Sent: December 10, 2004
To: My friends
CC: California
Subject: Send us some sun!

Friends,

Best wishes to all of you, and Happy New Year from the four of us! Our journey through the northwestern edge of the American nation is going through some extremely interesting twists and turns! I will send you an update soon.

I do have a small request for friends who live in California (or Singapore or Delhi). Can we trade our sun with yours for a few days? Ours has become very moody in the past couple of months.

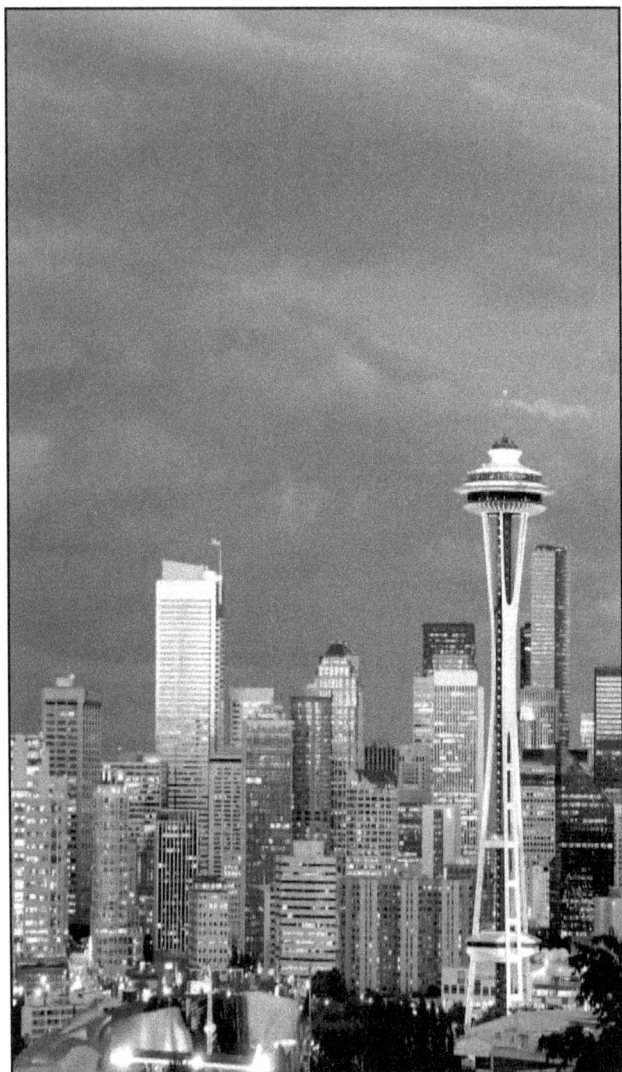

Seattle's gray sky during the 8-month-long gray season,
photo by Colin Zheng

During the summer, Seattle has one of the brightest and sunniest suns I have ever seen on three continents. It works long hours, shining brilliantly from 4 AM to 10 PM day after day.

Now, it appears to be de-motivated, as if it got all burned out or something. It is not shining. Instead, it hides behind those gray clouds, sipping mocha or a cappuccino. It does not show up for days! And when it finally does, it comes late to work, like at 9 AM, and goes back out at 4 PM. Slacker!

I am stumped. Maybe a change of work location will help?

But things are not all that bad here. No, really. It does not drizzle here all the time in fall, winter, and spring—only 90 percent of the time! And we do have sunny, cloudless days in winter, like, once every other week. Yes, those few cloudless days are freezing cold, but we would rather see the sky and be frozen than continue with that annoying drizzle.

So, California, can you send us your sun for a few days with the next batch of techies ditching you for Microsoft or Amazon? No, we don't want your traffic, your real estate pricing, or the governor Arnold Schwarzenegger. Thanks for the offer though. Just send us the sun!

Just for a few days? Please?

Me

PS: Not-So-Shy has turned three years old and has become even cuter! She is speaking and is bilingual, both English and Hindi! We also had our first snowfall in Northwest. Not-So-Shy could see it from her room and was so excited!

We wish you all Seasons Greetings and Happy Holidays!

Seattle's gray skies. Photo by Dr. Colin Zheng.

Firing Your Employer in Nine Easy Steps

Firing your employer can be a traumatic experience, but careful preparation can help things go more smoothly once the process is underway. No one can predict how an employer will react to the news that you have made alternate arrangements for your next paycheck. Some managers are surprised and tend to feel very guilty and remorseful. Others accept it more gracefully. Be ready for both cases and remain professional throughout the separation process. Make sure you maintain your dignity and respect for your manager. It's not his or her fault that the company could not create a work environment that kept you happy. Remember, it's a small world, and many of your past employers may be your next employer's customers. A poorly handled separation process could result in irreparable damage to your professional image.

At the same time, you don't need to feel guilty about leaving your employer. Remember, you had spent sixty to eighty hours a week at work and made personal sacrifices; in return, they needed to show you respect, increment your bank account at regular intervals, and give you interesting work. If an employer becomes incapable of meeting these needs, it is no longer entitled to your services, and the employee is free to look for another employer to meet those needs.

Here are the rules for this divorce-like process:

1. Do not discuss your decision to leave your employer with anyone at work until you find another job to replace your current job. (An exception may be a trusted colleague who has agreed to act as your character reference.)

2. Once you have found another employer who can do the job of employing you better than the current one, tender your resignation.

3. While talking to your manager, be polite but firm. No, they can't do anything to keep you

228 | Firing Your Employer in Nine Easy Steps

from leaving. It is too late for them to do anything about losing a star performer like you. During the exit interview with the human resources department of your current employer, consider giving the inside scoop on your manager.

4. Refuse to sign any additional paperwork they ask for when you leave. Remember, you already signed a lot of paperwork when you joined them. Now, they have no right to make you sign any more.

5. Carefully hand over any confidential information and company-owned property.

6. Send a partly funny, partly sentimental good-bye e-mail to everyone who is important or close to you at the workplace.

7. Chat gently with folks who come to say good-bye. Express sympathy because they are left behind and will continue to suffer.

8.   Accept the affectionate hugs or good-bye
       kisses offered by attractive colleagues of the
       opposite gender.

9.   Give your badge to your manager and leave.
       Don't look back.

After I handed over my badge and other crap to my
manager, I left the building and drove out onto the
freeway. Soon, I was on the bridge over Lake
Washington. It was the holiday season, the second-to-
the-last day of the year and there was no traffic.
Suddenly the enormity of it all hit me. Oh my God!
What have I done? I won't be getting the 10 percent
employee discount at Amazon anymore! That did it.
The dam broke. Yes, I broke into tears—but only for a
few seconds. The rational part of my brain, a man's
brain, had waited until no one was around for miles,
except the calm water below and the gray sky above,
before it let go and let the emotional side take over, for
thirty seconds.

Amazon, I had come to you to be part of a
revolution, to do something different, and to relive my

youth. It was real love, but you broke my heart. You turned out to be no different from other giant corporations and actually, you're much worse. At least Oracle and PeopleSoft did not pretend to be something other than profit-making machines. But you—you misled me. You lured me into thinking you were a revolution in the making. But you were just another machine—an enormous, emotionless conglomeration of calculating components, driven by metrics and numbers, devoid of all humanity, pushy and demanding, brutal and unkind. Once struck with this realization the flow of tears dried up.

The wind pushed out the clouds and a bright moon lit up the sky. I had crossed over into Bellevue and had left Seattle behind. The bright moon reminded me of my daughters' faces, which would light up when they see me. I pushed down on the gas pedal. I wanted to be with them.

In 28 hours, a new year would start and I would soon go to work as a senior vice president in a company thousands of miles away. A company that I hoped would allow me to express my own style, do my own thing, and dance to my own music.

The bridge was left behind, as was the water under it.

Moving
Again

The Inferno

That morning started as usual. I was driving my daughter to her school, as I have been doing for past 8 years. After driving for several miles, I started feeling a bit uncomfortable. Something had changed, something was different that day.

What? As I looked around, I noticed that the lush green hills of yesterday were replaced by dry looking canyons and steep ridges covered with bristly, brown and thirsty brushes; and the streets were lined up with houses with stucco exteriors uncomfortably close to each other. And in place of Seattle's thickly forests, the hill tops were jarred by rows upon rows of houses. Palm trees sprouted from every front yard and street corner. This wasn't Seattle! Seattle does not have palm trees.

Now, most people, when faced with a similar situation, wouldn't really know what to do -- but you know me, I'm a resourceful kind of a guy. I immediately took out my GPS equipped mobile phone, and looked up my location.

San Diego Convention Center

Say what? San Diego? I am back in California? Oh my God, how the hell did I get all the way from Seattle, Washington to San Diego?

Landing in San Diego (figuratively), Photo by Kalpanik S.

And why?

"Why am I here?" may appear to be a simple question; but answering it requires a deep study of religion, philosophy and science.

Is there a deeper purpose for us being where we are? Or is our location just a manifestation of the de-virtualization of our existence, sort of a corollary of Descartes' "cogito ergo sum" —I think (virtually), therefore I am (physically), and hence I have physical coordinates?

I pondered over these deep philosophical and scientific questions for the next few days, and dreamt that I was a quantum particle simultaneously existing everywhere in a 10 dimensional space-time multi-verse, with my wave function forced to collapse every time I had to specify my address.

If you were to be given a choice to be mysteriously transported somewhere else, most of you will perhaps not object too strongly to reappearing in San Diego .

San Diego Convention Center, Photo by Kalpanik S.

San Diego is best known for its beaches and mild,

pleasant climate, and rightfully so. We have a full

seventy miles of spectacular beaches, spread all the

way from our border with Riverside County on the

north to the Mexico border.

In addition, we also enjoy mild, sunny weather

throughout the year, with average monthly

temperatures ranging from about 57 °F(14 °C) to 72 °F(22 °C).

San Diego Beaches, Photo by Kalpanik S. featuring family members

A leading men's magazine, which I found in the seat pocket during a flight (I swear!); had declared San Diego's Mission Beach as the hottest beach in the world, rating it over beaches from Florida, France, Brazil and Bali.

San Diego's Beaches Are Hot! Stock Photo pruchased from Bigstock photos.

A visit to Mission Beach confirmed my suspicion that the learned editors of said literary publication were not exactly talking about its thermal properties.

And this particular attribute is not specific just to Mission Beach. In fact, no admirer of natural or feminine beauty is likely to be disappointed by a visit to any of the 20 or so beaches in San Diego. The fact that Southern California has the largest number of health food stores, personal trainers and cosmetic surgeons per capita in the world has probably as much to do with our climate and natural surroundings as it has to do with our wealth, vanity or pre-occupation with our appearance.

But everyone knows about San Diego's beaches; what took me by surprise was our semi-arid climate. San Diego has an annual rainfall of about 10 inches on average, making it the driest place I have ever lived in. Even Amman, Jordan gets 12 inches, and both Seattle and Nashville get more than 120 inches. In the six months I have been here, it hasn't rained even once.

This does mean, though, that we get a lot more sunny days. I guess as long as they keep piping us water from places as far as Colorado, we should be fine.

A Pier at San Diego Harbor, Photo by Colin Zheng

The other unusual thing in San Diego is its alternating pattern of deep canyons separating its mesas – a mesa is an elevated area of land with a flat top and sides that are usually steep cliffs.

These alternating mesas and canyons segment the city, creating physical gaps between otherwise proximal neighborhoods.

Our house is on top of such a mesa, overlooking a canyon.

The Inferno

Our semi arid climate combined with the strong Santa Ana winds that characteristically appear in Southern California during autumn and early winter make us very susceptible to wildfires.

In fact Shy, my elder daughter who studies environmental sciences, explained to us that wildfires are a natural and a necessary part of our ecosystem, and the plant species prevalent in our area have not only evolved to survive fires (by adaptations such as fire-resistant seeds), but some even encourage fires to eliminate their competition; for example, many species contain flammable oils in their leaves. All you need is a trigger, which could be natural, such as lightning, or human, such as sparks from power lines or ambers flying out from an innocuous barbeque, and pretty soon you have a blazing wildfire which can keep going for months.

This year, we had very little rain in the whole Southern California region, and only three inches in San Diego. The heat wave has dried out fallen branches, leaves and brush, making everything highly flammable.

It was Sunday, October 21st, and we were finally done with all the unpacking. I spent the day lazily reading a book, lying on a hammock in our backyard facing the canyon, enjoying our mild, sunny weather, and keeping a watchful eye on the swimming pools below [just in case someone started drowning and needed help ;-)]. Did I mention that we Southern Californians also have the largest number of swimming pools per capita in the world?

It was around 4:00 PM, a bit too early for the sun to lose its shine, but the sky had started becoming a bit hazy. Smog? I wondered. There was also a slight smell in the air, reminiscent of the polluted air on New Delhi's roads. Too many automobiles, I thought, and went inside, completely oblivious to the still invisible wildfire burning up there somewhere in the mountains.

An hour later, I habitually logged in, and saw an e-mail from our IS department alerting us about a fire in Ramona.

Fire? Ramona? I looked up the web-- Ramona, pop.30,000, described as a "bucolic mountain hamlet," is 20 miles northeast of us. There was no news about Ramona on the TV; but Malibu, the celebrity town, was on fire again.

Malibu, an oceanfront town, home to Britney Spears, Mel Gibson, Cher, Tom Hanks, Jennifer Aniston, Mel Brooks, Ryan O'Neal and many more, is almost always on fire every wildfire season. But it's 150 miles from here, making its celebrity fires too far to be risky for us.

Also, our IS department is very conscientious and, like Homeland Security, is always putting out alerts with various colors during the weekend. Usually, though, they're about computer services becoming temporarily unavailable or processes showing delays by a millisecond and such, so I didn't take the news too seriously; still, I did decide to keep monitoring things.

At 7:30 PM, there was another e-mail urging us to monitor TV, radio and internet updates because the fire in Ramona was growing larger. Almost at the same time, Shy told us that there was a strong smell of smoke in her room, which was the only room in the house that faced East.

Concerned a bit more, I turned on the TV again while simultaneously looking up the news on the internet. And this time, Ramona was indeed in the news. Many, but not all, of the 30,000 Ramonans were being evacuated.

The fire's location was 10 to 15 northeast of Ramona, making it 30 to 35 miles away from us.

They had set up an evacuation center in Poway High School. I reasoned that if they were evacuating people from Ramona to Poway, we should be safe because a fire in Ramona would need to cross the rest of Poway to get to us.

Also, the fire was reportedly burning in an area covering a few hundred acres, about 0.5 square miles. For it to cross 35 miles across rest of Poway and reach us, it would need to grow about 10,000 times its current size.

"Very unlikely," I thought.

At 9:30 PM, the phone rang, and an automated message from the Poway Unified School District announced that schools in the district would be closed the next day as a precautionary measure because of the high winds and high risk of wildfires.

This was a bummer, because my wife had just started working, so I would need to be at home. I e-mailed my colleagues and my manager that I would be working from home to look after the kids.

We watched the local news, and then slept through the night, not really worried about anything. After all, we had real natural disasters back in the Southeast, what with all the hurricanes, tornadoes and flash floods.

The phone started ringing at 6 am, waking us up. It was Clark, one of my colleagues. He asked me if we were all right. "What do you mean?" I asked. "Haven't you heard? Turn on the TV."

I did. Wow! The small brush fire which started 35 miles away from us less than 16 hours ago had grown into the largest wildfire currently burning in California. Dubbed the "Witch Creek" fire, it had blazed through 30 miles during the night, propelled by the mighty Santa Ana winds gusting more than 80 mph, and guided by our canyons and ridges, giving it pathways to travel.

Astonishingly, the fire had managed to "jump" across 16 lanes of I-15, about 5 miles north of us, the winds carrying the embers on their wings and dropping them on the other side, starting new fires. The freeway was shut down. A full 150 square miles were part of the "active burn area." People in most of Poway and the neighboring towns of Rancho Bernardo and Escondido were forced to evacuate, at minutes' notice in many cases.

Worse still, it was now accepted that there was no stopping this fire, that it would keep burning and going west until it hit the ocean, that the best we humble humans could do against the fury of mighty mother nature was to get out of its way and run for our lives. They had evacuated approximately 1800 squares miles, all the way to the beach communities of Del Mar and Solana Beach, asking a population of half a million to pack up and leave.

The large Qualcomm Stadium was opened up for the evacuees and several other evacuation centers were also opened.

And the Witch Creek fire, though now the largest wildfire burning in California and Mexico, was only one of three major fires in San Diego County and 18 other fires elsewhere in Southern California.

The current evacuation border was Highway 56, just a couple of miles north of us, so technically we were still outside the evacuation zone.

Officials had appealed to residents outside the evacuated areas to remain at home if possible, to keep highways clear for people who needed to leave and emergency vehicles, so we decided to stay home but started packing.

Important papers, passports, valuables, food, water and clothes for a few days, first aid kit, medicines, stuff for personal hygiene, books and magazines, sleeping bags. What else? Shy reminded Sonia to take a photo album. The car was packed full.

With Sonia protesting, I logged into work and checked on the whereabouts of my team -- many had already evacuated; some others, like me, were near the perimeter of evacuation in suburban townships, remaining in safe zones. By Monday afternoon, even larger areas of San Diego country were put on mandatory evacuation and finally, it was our turn to become part of the statistics.

There were 7 different "fires" burning by Monday in San Diego

The only hotel where I could get a room was just outside the current evacuation perimeter; I still preferred that over going to Qualcomm Stadium which was now housing 12,000 people.

President Bush had declared Southern California a disaster area, and Federal troops and assets were starting to join the evacuation and firefighting efforts.

But the indomitable, burly Santa Ana wind with its wings of fire kept propelling the infernos through the canyons and valleys. The seemed determined to exterminate us once and for all, clearing nature's sacred sanctuaries of our impudent, ugly nests, punishing us for audacious intrusion.

You could see flames bursting into the sky and dark ominous clouds of smoke rising at some distance in almost all directions; the sky was hazy, like it is at early morning, even in the middle of the day.

They had asked to conserve the electricity, since San Diego had lost many of the transmission lines bringing us power so even though it was 95 degrees outside, we turned off the air conditioning.

What would the night bring? Was this the end? What were our options? San Diego was running out of safe places. One of the freeways heading north was closed, the other jammed with evacuees. Even in normal circumstances, traffic towards LA is horrendous; now, we could spend 24 hours just on the freeway. Besides, the LA area had fires of its own.

To the east was mostly desert and taking that direction would mean going all the way to Las Vegas, mostly through internal roads. Being new to the area, I wasn't too familiar with the highways connecting us with nearby cities.

Or we could go down to Mexico, and spend some days there. But what if the Harris fire blocked the freeways going South?

We slept very apprehensively and lightly. We had left everything in the car except for some toothbrushes, food, and night clothes; we were mentally prepared to re-evacuate at a moment's notice.

By Wednesday morning, the Witch Creek fire had burned 300 square miles, though it did not spread beyond the areas already evacuated.

Additional firefighters arrived from the rest of California and other states, increasing the number of firefighters fighting the infernos in the to 9,000 -- 6,000 of them in San Diego alone.

The National Guard had arrived, and more firefighting planes and helicopters were brought in overnight from other states, including an unmanned plane from NASA. So far, 350,000 households -- a million people, 1/3 of the population of San Diego County -- had to leave their homes, making this the largest evacuation in the history of California.

By Wednesday afternoon, the fierce Santa Ana winds started calming down. Mother Nature finally decided to forgive us, and pretended to give in to the combined aerial and ground assault by firefighters.

Work resumed on Wednesday, and 70% of the people showed up, even though many of us were still evacuees. We were given the option of wearing breathing masks at work, to protect us from air "quality problems" (i.e., smoky air).

Lunch was brought in; there was a lot of black humor. One of the Vice Presidents had shown up at another's house with a trailer full of horses. One of the other colleagues shared her disappointment -- she was in a safe zone, so she had cleaned up her house and prepared extra food, well prepared to extend her hospitality to those in need, but even though she knew a lot of people in the evacuation areas, no one came. I promised her that we would show up for dinner during the weekend so that she can exercise her "hospitality" instinct.

Our neighborhood was opened up on Wednesday, though the schools remained closed for the whole week.

By Thursday, the strong Santa Ana winds were replaced by the cooler breezes from the ocean, flowing in the opposite direction and cooling the region, further shrinking the fires. The rest of the evacuated areas were slowly opened to residents on Thursday and Friday, though National Guardsmen were accompanying people in some areas. There were long traffic lines in many areas.

As the air cooled down, all the ash particles lifted miles into the atmosphere started slowly sinking, filling our valleys with an ominous, dark fog and making our sky hazy; places hundreds of miles from the burn sites were warned about potential air quality problems.

Qualcomm Stadium was closed on Friday, and the remaining evacuees, now down to a few hundred, were moved to several smaller centers. All three major fires were still burning, and were expected to continue to do so through the first week of November, but they had much smaller footprints.

Residents were finally allowed to return to their homes in Ramona, where our little wildfire started, on Friday afternoon, but they had no water and, in many cases, no electricity. Fire trucks that had sucked up 300 gallons at a time had drained the town's reservoir.

As of Friday afternoon, the wildfires had killed at least 12 people, had blackened some 800 square miles of Southern California, and had destroyed 2,000 homes and other structures. Losses were expected to top $1 billion in hardest-hit San Diego County alone.

But we escaped mostly unscathed, unlike many others. The only cleanup we had to do was scrubbing a bathtub which got some ash deposited in it because of an open window. Apart from breathing some smoky air for five days, the psychological trauma my daughter Not-So-Shy suffered when I grimly apprised her of the possibility that her school "Shoal Creek Elementary" may have to be renamed to "Coal Creek Elementary," and having to closely monitor two mini natural disasters (our kids) for a week because their schools were closed, we suffered no major harm.

Not-so-shy wonders if her school may now be renamed from Shoal Creek
Elementary to Coal Creek Elementary. Photo by Kalpanik S.

Kindle Kindles a Flame of Creativity

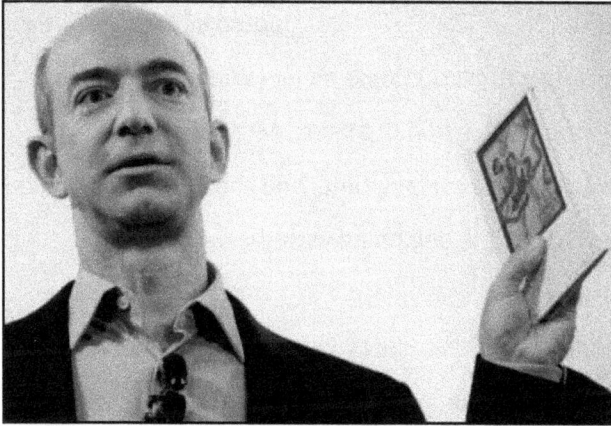

Jeff Bezos introduces the Kindle in 2007. Reprinted under the fair use doctrine as permitted by Section 107 of the U.S. Copyright Act.

In November 2007, three years after I had left Amazon, Newsweek featured Jeff Bezos on its cover, holding a gizmo in his hand. The cover story described a revolution in the book industry. It claimed that, "Amazon's Jeff Bezos already built a better bookstore. Now he believes he can improve upon one of humankind's most divine creations: the book itself."

Build an electronic book? So Amazon was getting into hardware and taking on a media form—the printed book—which has refused to become obsolete for over 4,000 years?

In the article, Bezos was quoted as saying, "The book just turns out to be an incredible device. Books are the last bastion of analog. Music and video have been digital for a long time, and short-form reading has been digitized, beginning with the early Web. But long-form reading really hasn't." At least, not so far. The Kindle was dubbed Book 2.0, mimicking the Web 2.0 terminology, and was not only expected to change the way readers read, but also how writers write and publishers publish. Bezos was about to force the publishing world to take a quantum leap into the world of digitalized creativity.

To make the Kindle, Amazon had to get into designing and manufacturing a product rather than simply selling it. Lab 126 in Cupertino, California—the home of Apple— was set up to develop the new product. Apple Inc. veteran, Greg Zehr, was hired as one of Kindle's main engineers. Other hires came from

Palm, Hewlett-Packard, Motorola, and Microsoft. Bezos, who is an avid reader, understood that to make Kindle successful, a new technology would be needed that addressed the current disadvantages of reading a book on a portable electronic device, so he hired engineers with experience in all of the major forms of portable computers.

It was already possible to read an electronic book on handheld computers, but ease of reading for long periods of time, especially outdoors, was a major reason why readers refused to adopt electronic books. The other major issue was that handheld computers had no book-like capabilities such as easily flipping through the pages and adding a bookmark. When compared to reading an electronic book, a hardcopy book was a vastly superior experience. The development team at Lab 126 had to create a device that made the experience of reading a book electronically superior to that of the traditional book experience. And once that was achieved, publishers would naturally begin to provide books in digital formats.

Initially, I had mixed feelings about Amazon's venture into the design and manufacture of hardware. While there have been some nice examples of companies being able to cross the hardware/software divide—for example, Microsoft with its Xbox—I considered these examples to be exceptions to the rule. In most cases, companies that tried to foray across the hardware/software divide have failed. But my experience with the first Kindle was very encouraging. Though it had been widely referred to as the iPod of the book, I found Kindle to be far superior to an iPod. Kindle had solved a major problem with iPod and portable MP3 players—it eliminated the requirement of hooking up, or synchronizing with, a computer. Yes, no computer required! And the wireless subscription was free.

Amazon had done a great job of lining up content. In addition to books, most of the popular newspapers and magazines were available on the Kindle, including The New York Times, LA Times, Wall Street Journal, Washington Post, Forbes, Fortune, and Time; and blogs such as TechCrunch, Motley Fool, Huffington Post, and

BoingBoing. Those of you who are reading this book on a Kindle know that none of the content, not even the blogs, is free (at least not yet). However, you must admit that the smaller form of Kindle, combined with the fact that you can read a book or a blog without being connected to the Internet, does make it easier to read while on a plane or the subway.

The Kindle became the cool high-tech Christmas gift for 2007 and it has continued to be the most popular and gifted product on Amazon year after year. But the biggest benefit Kindle brought to me was not in reading books. By simplifying the publishing process and bringing it within my reach, Kindle kindled a creative flame in me. I had been informally writing about my experiences for the last twenty-three years, since I came to the United States on a scholarship to study computer engineering at the University of California. I had been sharing those pieces with friends—initially, believe it or not, using snail mail, then via e-mail, and then on the Web. I had been too busy to follow the traditional publishing path and had instinctively known that the market for a book about the experiences of a foreign-born technologist was rather limited.

But suddenly, publishing a book was easily within my reach. All I needed to do was combine those various pieces, fill in the gaps, polish the material, and hire an editor. Amazon has made it easy for authors to self-publish their work by accepting a wide variety of file formats, including those from Microsoft Word. Also, the process of releasing a book was similar to releasing software—with frequent updates, based on the feedback from readers and the availability of time. A writer can upload a new master every month or, if he or she really wanted to, every week or even every two to three days.

My first book, Artificial Imagination, was about my experiences while living in various places in the United States beginning with my arrival as a student. It was published on January 7, 2008. Two years later I published a book about my experiences at Amazon, and the first edition of *Inside the Giant Machine: An Amazon.com Story* was published in March 2010. The tremendous success of the first edition surprised me, though a frequent feedback from readers was that they wanted to see more details, and so I decided on a second edition.

No discussion of Kindle in 2010 would be complete without mentioning Apple's iPad, as well as Google's foray into digital book distribution through the Google Editions program. After Kindle's successful adoption by the public, Apple's CEO Steve Jobs was quoted in *The New York Times* in January 2008 saying, "It doesn't matter how good or bad the product is, the fact is that people don't read anymore." However, Jobs did a 360-degree turn around and countered the Kindle with the iPad, though he claimed that development of the iPad was begun before the Kindle came out and its launch was delayed only in order to release the very successful iPhone first.

In addition to functioning as an e-book reader, the iPad offers applications and color graphics. While the major publishers want sales on any platform, many deliberately waited to invest in order to see what additional capabilities the iPad would offer for their books. In an interview with *The New York Times* on September 9, 2009, Steve Jobs said, "I'm sure there will always be dedicated devices, and they may have a few advantages in doing just one thing. But I think the general-purpose devices will win the day. Because I think people just probably aren't willing to pay for a dedicated device."

Google also joined the foray into the digital distribution of books with the launch of Google Editions, which includes digital books in both PDF and EPUB format. While the Amazon Kindle has taken a proprietary approach to digital book formats similar to Apple's approach on the iPod, Google has adopted the EPUB standard, which is an open format. The EPUB format for books is analogous to the MP3 format for music. Google launched its online digital bookstore with 500,000 books—an impressive number by any measure, but still less than the 750,000 titles available for Kindle. Nonetheless, Google is a serious threat to Amazon. With Google Editions, people can easily access the contents of electronic books on a variety of platforms.

Google used the divide-and-conquer strategy to establish its place in the world of electronic books, which was, at that time, largely dominated by Amazon's Kindle and Apple's iPad. Google trumped Amazon with its strategy to make the ecosystem of electronic books more open by making them available through Google or any other online retailer. Google books are also accessible through many web-based services on PDA phones, PCs, and tablets. This starkly contrasts with the Amazon's Kindle ecosystem, where people can order their books only through Amazon's store. In addition, Google avoids the use of intermediaries, giving people direct access to their web library. In contrast, people have to download the Kindle application to be able to read Kindle books on their computers or Smart phones.

There are reports that Google has already inked deals with some of the major publishers in the industry and plans to sell millions of books at prices that match or beat Amazon's. If this is true, Google's strategy will place it right beside Amazon. Obviously, with the majority of searches being done on Google, the search engine company can use that to its advantage; putting Google Editions books at the top of the search results.

Google planned to scan all of the 150 million books that have been published in the world for their searchable library, but authors and publishers responded with a class action suit alleging that Google's plan was a colossal case of copyright infringement. In 2008, Google reached a settlement with authors and publishers, paying $125 million to copyright owners, publishers and attorneys. In addition, some of the settlement money was used to create the Books Rights Registry, which provides the copyright owners with a share of book sales, revenues, and subscriptions. Problems with the joint venture in the initial agreement surfaced quickly and in 2009, the parties in the lawsuit amended the agreement to include policies on foreign works, orphan works and licenses for public libraries, as well as adjusting the revenue model to allow the copyright owners to renegotiate their revenue shares. Google is also developing an affiliate program that will provide online retailers with revenue-sharing opportunities by recommending e-books included on Google Editions.

The terms of the settlement have generated a lot of criticism throughout the publishing industry and it remains to be seen whether Google has won the war to obtain the right to control virtually every book on earth. However, it is clear that Google has successfully identified the weaknesses in Amazon's model for Kindle and is boldly exploiting them in the competition for the electronic book market.

A Book about Amazon, by Amazon, on Amazon

If you are reading a printed version of the book, Amazon printed it. Amazon publishes books under the business name CreateSpace and based on the previous sales, there is 30-40% chance that you bought this book about Amazon, published by Amazon, on Amazon.com. Unlike everyone else, who were taking the print version of their books and making them available on Kindle, I went the other way. I published my books on Kindle first, and then made the decision for a print version.

The motivation for publishing my books in print was two-fold. First, I was pleasantly surprised to see Artificial Imagination get to the top 2 percent in sales ranks among Kindle books—and it stayed there for a while. I guess the early adopters of Kindle were people who love gadgets and were apt to like the title

"Artificial Imagination," which refers to the simulation of imagination by computers. Secondly, I wanted to see all the amazing photographs of Seattle and San Diego taken by my co-contributor, Dr. Colin Zheng, in color. Kindle, in spite of all of its strengths, only shows photographs in black and white.

Once again, Amazon made the transition to a different media format easy. Amazon operates a self-publishing service dubbed CreateSpace. CreateSpace is a subsidiary of Amazon, which allows creative artists—musicians, filmmakers, and authors—to publish their music, videos, and books using an on-demand manufacturing and delivery model. Not every individual book, CD or DVD is literally printed on demand. Amazon manufactures a very small number of copies to keep on hand as inventory in their warehouse. As the product in the warehouse sells and its inventory falls below a certain trigger, additional copies of the book, CD or DVD are manufactured and sent to the warehouse.

The limits that CreateSpace places on its books are surprisingly tolerant. CreateSpace books must be paperback and must have color covers printed at 300-dpi resolution. Books can be printed in any of twelve different trim sizes, from five-by-eight inches to eight-by-ten inches. The system automatically classifies the interior of books into all-black-and-white or all-color. Consultants are available to help new authors in editing and in cover design as they put their book together, and in marketing the book after it is published. Independent musicians and filmmakers are able to use CreateSpace in the same way. Amazon's publish-on-demand technology is the extreme case of the just-in-time inventory system made popular by Wal-Mart.

Time magazine claims that since the introduction of CreateSpace, more than half of all titles published in the United States are now self-published. In an interview with Fortune magazine, Bezos said the Amazon publishing models, including both Kindle publishing and CreateSpace, empower both authors and small publishers.

After I submitted this book, one of their diligent customer service representatives challenged my right to include some of the photos, which are legally reproduced without permission under the fair use doctrine, as permitted under section 107 of the U.S. Copyright Act. I had to send them more than 125 pages of legal documents. After reviewing those, Amazon conceded to my right to reproduce all of the one hundred or so photographs and agreed to continue to print, sell, and distribute this book.

Here are excerpts from the email exchange with names masked to protect the privacy of the persons involved. (Note: CreateSpace is an assumed name or DBA, which stands for "doing business as", of Amazon—a legal way for a company to do business under another name):

Dear Kalpanik,

My name is XXXX with CreateSpace Executive Customer Relations and I would like to thank you for choosing CreateSpace to distribute your title(s). I am contacting you regarding the following title(s):

1. "Inside the Giant Machine - An Amazon.com Story: Color Interior Edition," title ID 3438387

2. "Inside the Giant Machine: An Amazon.com Story," title ID 3437797

In order to ensure the works we distribute do not violate the rights of others (such as copyright and privacy), we are required to verify that you, the content provider, are authorized to distribute the title(s) and the content within it. Please reply with confirmation of such rights and/or permissions to publish the title(s) and provide any documentation or other evidence of these rights and/or permissions.

Specifically, please provide us with such rights and/or permissions regarding the images used within these titles that may be under copyright protection through other sources. For example, please provide us with such relevant information regarding the images so that we may move forward with the title(s). Please reply to XXX@createspace.com with your confirmation and with appropriate documentation of your rights and/or permissions for your title(s) within two weeks from the date of this e-mail. If we do not receive such information by Tuesday, March 23, 2010, the title(s) will be moved to a retired status through CreateSpace, making them unavailable for new manufacture. We thank you in advance for your attention to this.

Sincerely,

XXXX

Executive Customer Relations

I responded to the above with 125 pages of documents. My collaborator, Dr. Colin Zheng, took most of the photos in the book, some by were taken by

me or other friends, and a few, such as the book cover,
were purchased from stock photo websites. A handful
was reproduced without permission under the fair use
doctrine, as permitted by section 107 of the U.S.
Copyright Act.

Here is a sample document I sent them:

Ms. Lopez's curvature can be
modeled using a hyperbolic
paraboloid, as depicted below.

I, ▮▮▮▮▮▮▮ a photo-journalist believe I have rights to use this image of Ms. J.
Lopez along with the drawing of a Hyperbloic paraboloid under the fair use doctrine –
the photo has been converted to black and white (Even though it targeted for
publication in a color book), has been reduced to a fairly small size (1 inch X 1 inch on
a 7 inch X 10 inch page), and is being used with a scientific drawing for the purpose
of illustrating a mathematical topology in conjunction with a technical description. This
1 inch X 1 inch depiction of Ms. J. Lopez is not a main feature of the book by any means
and there is no direct or implied endorsement of any kind by Ms. J. Lopez. Hence I
believe under the United States copyright laws, I have rights to use this image under the
fair use doctrine as part of the Interior File of my book "Inside the Giant Machine- An
Amazon.com story" written under my pen name, Kalpanik S.

Signed March 14th

▮▮▮▮▮▮▮

After a thorough review of 125 pages of such
assertions, Amazon agreed to continue to print on

demand, sell, and distribute this book. Their response marked a victory for the freedom of the press:

Hi Mr. Kalpanik,

I am connecting with you to provide an update on the images within your titles. After our review of the documentation provided, we will be moving forward with these titles as usual, and will continue to publish, sell and distribute them. Thank you again for your cooperation and taking the time to work with us. Should you have any questions in the future, please don't hesitate to contact me. Have a wonderful weekend.

Sincerely,

XXXXX

Executive Customer Relations

Phew! This came as a relief and even somewhat of a surprise – I was pretty sure that Amazon will try to nix at least some photos, specially the photo of Ms. Lopez. But Amazon stayed true to being neutral and non-judgmental for content I have to say that even though I did not care much for Amazon as an employer, I do like them as the on-demand publisher, distributor and seller for my book on Amazon.

Feminization of Las Vegas in Early 21st Century

Note: the author, a noted urban anthropologist (among other things) does not drink, smoke or gamble; his annual expeditions to Las Vegas are purely for the purpose of scientific research.

Las Vegas, 16 April 2009

After I handed over my federal and state tax returns to the post office worker at 6:59 PM on April 15, I realized it was time to make my bi-annual trip to Las Vegas. My last trip was in August of 2008, so with 20 months gone, it was about time to make another scientific expedition.

I packed my bag and drove, stopping only when I reached my observation post.

I like to observe Las Vegas at the "The Strip". It has fascinated me since the first time I visited it in 1987, as part of a research team consisting of graduate students from the University of California. It was my third month in America and Las Vegas was a nice introduction to the glittery side of the United States. Since then, I have been visiting it every two years on the average.

I started my customary observation of The Strip starting at the south end. Some of the changes on the Strip were obvious. There were now a series of really tall steel and glass towers in front of MGM and behind New York New York.

After walking for about 20 minutes, I started to get an eerie feeling. You know, that feeling you feel when you are feeling the feeling that something is out of order, but you are unable to pin it down.

After a few more minutes, it came to me. There were more females than males walking on the strip! And not just a few more females, but significantly more! Did I notice this because my females, my wife and two daughters, had been away for past three weeks visiting my in-laws? Or was there a truth in what I was seeing?

Being a scientist, I decided to follow the scientific

method to answer this question. I would take random population samples on and around The Strip. I stopped every two minutes, taking random counts (samples) of people within 10 yards of me. I ignored the couples and only counted men or women walking solo or in groups.

After taking eight counts at different places —four on the Strip, one inside a souvenir shop, one in CVS, one inside a restaurant and the final one at the yogurt shop in Aria, the new upscale hotel—the results were fairly consistent. Excluding the couples, on average the women outnumbered men 2-to-1!

Hmm, was there a shoe sale at the shopping complex in the Venetian?

A quick googling on my Blackberry showed no shoe sales at Venetian, but my hunch was partly right. In addition to shoes, there were handbags, belts and other luxury leather goods available. Right there, on the Strip, was a large Louis Vuitton store. In case you're not familiar with Louis Vuitton, it is a French leather goods shop, a place to go if you want to shell out a thousand dollars on a handbag or a pair of shoes.

And next to Louis Vuitton was Tiffany's and Saks Fifth Avenue. The Fashion Mall nearby housed two Macys stores, a Nordstrom's and another 250 high-end stores. And if that wasn't enough, all eight of the new five-star hotels had their own mini-shopping complexes inside!

In the past, the shopping at Las Vegas was hidden in the mega-complexes at the Venetian Canal shops and under the Caesar's Palace artificial sky. Both of those have a theme, so shopping was portrayed as more of a byproduct of creating that special effect.

But now, the luxury shops with handbags, shoes, clothing and jewelry were boldly placed right on the Strip! The Strip was no longer a place where gentlemen went to have a quiet drink to wash down their pain and suffering in silent communion with other gentlemen while gathered around a round stage with a bulbous specimen of the human species contorting her body around a pole. It had become a place where one went to buy designer handbags and shoes.

Brothers, I have bad news for you! It gets worse, much worse.

A closer look at the new hotels on the south end, the Vdara, Palazzio, THEhotel, the Mandarin Oriental and the Aria, revealed another sinister transformation the City of Sin had undergone. In the two years since I had been here last, all of the eight new hotels call themselves a "Hotel and Spa". No, no more "Hotel and Casino", now it is "Hotel and Spa".

And they are not lying. A visit to Mandarin Oriental showed how serious these "Hotels and Spas" were about the spa business. The Mandarin Oriental has a full 27,000 square feet spread over two levels that is dedicated to Moroccan mud treatments, Thai Aromatic body wraps, facials, Chinese foot massages and waxing arms, armpits, legs, and other unmentionable body areas.

The City of Sin had turned overnight into the City of Spas! I could feel Billy Wilkerson and Benjamin Siegel turn in their graves.

Handbags, shoes, body treatment, waxing—what else? I shuddered with fear and horror as I learned that there were now five art museums, each challenging the $100 million collection at the Venetian. What the heck? This is not Paris, it's Las Vegas! We don't need those darned art museums here!

Las Vegas is no longer a city for gentlemen who need to escape the reality of their harsh lives by gambling, smoking cigars and drinking hard liquor. Las Vegas is where you go when you want a pedicure, a manicure or a mud bath. It's a place to buy handbags and to visit museums.

In fact, the meaning of both the words "drink" and "club" had changed. The drink was no longer a dark brown liquid served in a short glass. It was not even the traditional "shaken, not stirred" martini. A "drink" had become a colorful, pink, red or green concoction served in a tall fancy container shaped like the Eiffel Tower or a cute bear or some other fancy shape that no guy would ever be caught drinking out of. A drink in a tall plastic Eiffel tower! Shudder!

And the club was no longer a place where gentlemen in suits and serious, serene faces went to commune with other gentlemen to understand the meaning of life by sipping some ugly brown brew out of a glass and staring at voluptuous women stripping themselves in the center. No sir, the club in Las Vegas was now a place where women, dressed in fashionable clothing and high heels, gathered to chat with their girl friends while drinking colorful pink drinks and giggling. Yes, a club in Vegas was now a scene right of the *Sex and the City*. It was obvious that Las Vegas was now aspiring to be Times Square, Paris and a Mediterranean resort rolled into one!!

Sigh, Las Vegas was no longer the joint where I could go to when I felt oppressed by the female majority in my household. Even though I don't drink, gamble or smoke, and it has been more than a decade since I have visited a "gentlemen's club" in Las Vegas (or anywhere else for that matter); just walking on the strip and enjoying the rare male majority gave my morale a boost.

I returned to Southern California with a heavy heart the next day.

An alarming new statistic shows that males are becoming a minority in the US. A linear projection of the last 50 years reveals a decrease in the male percentage of the population (now at 49%). It projects that men will be extinct in the United States in a mere 5,000 years. Drastic steps for the conservation of men must be taken right now! Write to your congresswoman today. And treat your men kindly and gently. You need them to kill spiders, take out the garbage, fix the car, and to carry heavy objects.

Works Cited

Daisey, Mike. *21 Dog Years : Doing Time @ Amazon.com.* Free Press, 2002.

Frost, Robert. *Stopping by Woods on a Snowy Evening.* 1923.

Grossman, Lev, and Andrea Sachs. "Is Amazon Taking Over the Book Business?" *Time*, June 22, 2009.

Levy, Steven. "The Future of Reading." *Newsweek*, November 17, 2007.

Marcus, James. *Amazonia: Five Years at the Epicenter of the Dot.Com Juggernaut .* The New Press, 2004.

Markoff, John. "The Passion of Steve Jobs." *The New York Times*, January 15, 2008.

O'Brien, Jeffrey M. "Amazon's next revolution." *Fortune*, May 26, 2009.

Pogue, David. "Steve Jobs on Amazon and Ice Cream." *The New York Times*, September 9, 2009.

S., Kalpanik. *I Met A Greek Goddess In Nashville.* Center of Artificial Imagination, Inc., 2008.

Spector, Robert. *Amazon.com: Get Big Fast.* Harper Paperbacks, 2002.

Toffler, Alvin. *Future Shock.* Bantam, 1984.

Vogelstein, Fred. "Mighty Amazon Jeff Bezos." *Fortune*, May 26, 2003.

.

www.ingramcontent.com/pod-product-compliance
Lightning Source LLC
Chambersburg PA
CBHW051944090426
42741CB00008B/1258